MW00804892

Opening the Vermillion Spirit

打开朱红色的精神

Folk Necromancy in Transmission, VOLUME 6

OPENING

the

Vermillion Spirit

JOHN ANDERSON

Revelore

OLYMPIA, WA

MMXXI

Opening the Vermillion Spirit

© John Anderson 2021.

Sixth volume of the Folk Necromancy in Transmission series conceived and curated by Dr Alexander Cummins and Jesse Hathaway Diaz.

All rights reserved. No part of this publication may be reproduced or utilized in any form or by any means, electronic or mechanical, including photocopying, recording, or by any information storage and retrieval system, without permission in writing from the Publishers.

Book and cover design by Joseph Uccello.
Cover art by Bryan Paul Patterson, 2020.

ISBN 978-1-947544-30-7

Printed globally on demand through IngramSpark

First printed by Revelore Press in 2021

Revelore Press
620 73rd Ave NE
Olympia, WA 98506
United States

www.revelore.press

Contents

It's hard to be a human being.

—NORMAN LEAR

FOREWORD

I have been heartily recommending Dr. John Anderson's *Way of the Living Ghost* since its publication. The reach of the text has thrilled me, but not surprised me. It has been a potent invitation to dialogue. His latest offering invites us onto a new stage of the path. John is creating a body of work that slips through the cracks, and bursts into being like mycelial fruit in a dark hollow: or like a vermillion bird that rises from the depths of the Northern waters to ascend unto the heights of the Southern reaches. We are reminded that the Sage always faces South in the classical Chinese worldview, and in this new text, John makes the critical turn from the path of the living ghost, to the communion, communication, and consanguinity with the Heart Spirit: the Shen. Taking the ontological turn, paradoxically is the path of return. Opening to the multiple, returns one to the unity within that multiplicity.

First there was the dark night of the way of the living ghost; the necessity of doing the shadow work, the nigredo, surrendering to the katabasis, and diving into the depths. But it is through the return to primal waters, that the red bird awakens and discovers its longing to move against the force of gravity in its longing to fly, and fully express itself. It is the passage through the wending of the Wood phase and the primeval renewal of Spring that the drive to awakening is realized. This is also the force of the circulation in the human being: the movement of the Blood.

There is another more substantive model of Blood in Chinese medicine that describes the products of nutrition assuming the stamp of the Heart and its spirit, the Shen. It is a meeting between power and substance, which can create a suitable vessel for the transmission of the spirits. There is a dialogue between these two aspects that come to define Blood: and much of the magic inherent in John's writing emerges in a dialectic.

Blood is a fit emblem for the project outlined in this book. The rubedo that reveals itself in circulation is the essence that becomes the offering to the spirits. John offers a number of practices in the text that transform into rituals that guide one back to the path of the humane, and bring one into contact with the primary resources of embodiment. What is so extraordinary about the Chinese bio-psycho-spiritual model that informs John's work is that it both recognizes the cycles inherent within the vital circulation, and indeed, within life and the cosmos alike, as well as perceiving the fugitive escapes that open the circle into a spiral. In Su Wen, Chapter 26, we read that "Yin and yang [qì] mingle with each other; true [qì] and evil [qì] are not separate."[1] That is the meaning of the triad presented by Blood circulation, Blood as prima materia, and Blood as the cypher for the Heart; circulation, substance, and Spirit are not separate. The quality that admits of this multiplicity, again, guides one back to its unity, and creates an opening into further intensifications, and becoming.

Dr. John Anderson invites us to open our eyes, and hearts in this wonderful offering, but in a vein that might described by this passage from Su Wen, Chapter 26:

> The spirit! Ah, the spirit! The ears do not hear it. When the physician's eyes are clear, their heart is open and their mind goes ahead. They alone apprehend [it as if it were] clearly per-

---

1 Paul Unschuld, (ed.), *Huang Di nei jing su wen: An Annotated Translation of Huang Di's Inner Classic-Basic Questions* (Berkeley: University of California Press, 2011), 436.

ceivable. But the mouth cannot speak [of it]. Everyone looks, but they alone see. If one approaches it, it seems obscure [but to them] alone it is obvious [as if it were] clearly displayed. As if the wind had blown away clouds, hence one speaks of spirit.[2]

The path of return illuminated here is one aspect of realizing that a state of immediate concretization is precisely through an increasing state of wakeful presence that is necessarily embodied: concretization of the spiritual is embodiment. And the body brings us back to ourselves, back to Life.

Brandt Stickley, L.Ac
Assistant Professor
College of Classical Chinese Medicine
National University of Natural Medicine
PORTLAND, OREGON

2 Unschuld, *Huang Di nei jing su wen*, 445.

Introduction

The Emperor sits on his throne and does little else. His decrees are all the issues forth, and these are carried out by his subjects. If the Emperor is in good health, and provides for his people, he is imbued with the power of heaven.

The Red Bird takes flight. Movements swiftly and smoothly toward the South. It carries in its beak a seed. The seed which will become a nation. This gift only given after it is taken in by the cosmic mother who will safeguard these people within her own self until such time as they are ready to be born.

The heart (Xīn; 心) keeps its steady paces, drumming within the ears, it is nothing less than the drumming of Heaven. The Heart-mind (also Xīn; 心) keeps its steady paces, the paces of You. This is the enlivened heart—less a mechanism and more a mansion.

A mansion for the Shén spirit.

A resting place, a nesting place for the Red Bird.

A throneseat for the Vermillion Cinnabar spirit within.

When the heart alights properly, and blood flows through the vessels, there is life. When the life-giving, ever-moving essence that is the Blood ceases its continuous circuit, there is death. In the first instance, we find the nexus of the indwelling spirits, at once at home and also Other, and one of the keys to Human-ness. In the second, we find the abode of ghosts, who have lost much of their Human-ness, and who are estranged even unto themselves.

The following text is written for those of us who find ourselves caught at a crossroads. At one turn, we might become ambassadors of our own inertia—caught and subtly blinded by our own histories and choices both made and ignored.

The Way of the Living Ghost presents the reader with the means toward ghostliness, and this is one of the more startling implications be had from it—that many of us, perhaps even most of us, are but ghosts in-waiting.

The present text provides a means toward an alternate future, the seedling possibility of another story for ourselves and the world around us. It posits a world that is filled with the unseen, spirits of both light and dark, and encourages interaction there. More than this, though, the reader is asked to engage with the whole of the world including other human beings. This is no less the same, as human beings, too, are beings populated by spirits according to the cosmos of the greater Chinese tradition, just as the "external" world is filled with a great many unseen forces, supernatural and otherwise.[1]

*　*　*

Finding the Open Way

Whereas the way of the living ghost is often crooked and fraught with pressure, hunger, and clinging, its counter—the way of the human—is to look for spaces of openness, of freedom, of expression, of contentedness, and of awareness. It would be a mistake however to assume that this open path is one of necessary ease and/or beauty. To enter into the way of the Tao is simple enough, but to reside there is often quite difficult. The Tao is asymmetrical and always moving. Even the ideas of Yin and Yang are human ideas, a highly arbitrary division. They therefore provide no inherent steady ground, save for that which we take time to work with.

This text is nonlinear, and need not be read in particular order. An effort has been made to make each one of the passages its own self-contained essay. Even still, one will want to read carefully, as context for the ideas represented here is dispersed widely throughout the book.

This text, the one that precedes it, and the one which will follow it are all animist in their approach. That is to say that the body-composite, the psyche-composite, and the cosmos-writ-large which each

---

1 The term "supernatural" is something of a misnomer within any currents of both the Taoist and Buddhist traditions. In a broad sense, all spirits, whether "good" or "evil" have a reality that conforms to the ordering principle of heaven (Tianli). Through this order, each is thusly rendered "natural," even if they are marvelous, odd, or uncanny in presence.

of us expresses according to Daoism and other curren
thought, are, to a great extent, alive and possess both a
tion which are very often outside of our own awareness
ate control. This approach openly accepts the murk, co
paradox that accompanies enlivened existence and in _
The state of the human as both spirit-filled and spirit-driven is granted, but the question arises as to what we mean though when we say
spirit or spirits within the context of self?

The Many Faces of "Spirit" in Chinese Culture

The many and varied ideas of spirit are used broadly across any discussion of esoteric matters, and this is no different in the Chinese historical context. There are three main terms in Chinese which can be
subsumed within the broader idea of "a spirit." Namely, these are the:

• Guǐ   • Líng   • Shén

The term "guǐ" (鬼) is used to represent certain types of entities, qualities, or events which possess a malicious (or at least pernicious) nature. Situations that are associated with the term are considered the
most Yin in nature; the term can encompass both the dead and the
living. This class of beings, and the use of the word in a phrase takes
on a negative connotation. We can see this in terms such as: yānguǐ
(烟鬼; a heavy smoker, chain smoker), sèguǐ (色鬼; a lech or a pervert),
and jiǔguǐ (酒鬼; a drunkard), as well as in the singular guǐ (ghost, demon, terrible, damnable, etc.). This class of beings tends to represent
restlessness and dis-ease.

Líng (靈) are a broad category of entities, situations, and phenomena running the gamut from the numinous to the mundane, and the
spirits associated with them. We see this word in terms such as: língyì
(靈異; deity, monster, strange, mysterious, supernatural), jīnglíng (精
靈; spirit, fairy, elf, sprite, genie), Shènglíng (聖靈; the Holy Ghost, the
Holy Spirit), and of course, líng (靈; quick, alert, and effective, as well
as spirit, departed soul, or coffin). We see in this classification beings
and qualities which refer to or which possess ephemeral qualities not

stuck in place and time in the same manner that ghosts often are.

The phenomena, entities, and qualities denoted by the term "líng" do not have to be human, and very often are used to denote entities tied to weather and terrestrial forms as well as being a broad space which can encompass, beings which are analogous to those liminal spirits which are akin to faeries, elves, or sprites. The concept of ling can therefore be used to cover vast imaginal spaces that include both light and dark even as they are seen to be relative to one another in Daoist philosophy.

The Shén-as-spirit tends to work in the space of light and lightness. They are those spirits which hold the "spiritual" fixed in humanity, and which interact with more diaphanous, if not overtly divine realms. The Shén as a class of spirits is recognizable, but some other definitions of Shén can be difficult to decipher, as the term encompasses a great many related ideas and warrants further elucidation.

The Concept of "Shén" (神)

The concept of "shén" (神) lies at the crux of any discussion of psyche, cosmology, and metaphysics of Chinese culture. Its use and meanings are widespread, and it is also one of the most difficult ideas to parse out for modern readers. Modern definitions of the term shén include:[2]

- Deity
- Soul
- Spirit
- Unusual
- Mysterious
- Lively
- Expressive
- Countenance
- Look (the visual appearance of a thing)
- Amazing

2 https://chinese.yabla.com/chinese-english-pinyin-dictionary.php?define=shen

As can be evinced from even this short list, the associated fields of meaning are broad, and can therefore encompass a vast swath of experience. From a classical perspective, the definitions which lie toward the end of this list, such as countenance, lively, amazing, etc., stem from the action or actions attributed to souls and/or spirits as epiphenomena of interrelated consequence: when one's spirit or soul is well cared for, one is more likely to exhibit a "brightness" of being (Míng, 明) which shines through in the eyes and in the warmth of one's general expression.

As a spirit form, the Shén of the Heart is considered the clearest, most ephemeral of the Five Shén (Wushén; 五神) and, it is fair to say, the spirit with the strongest affinity for sacred affairs and works, and also the most essential for the fullest expression of the cosmic principles which lie at the center of many of the varied cosmologies of Asia.

Why is this?

In a word: connection.

These are the Three Realms according to the Daoist worldview, and it is the unique capacity of the Heart to take in material and to go forth by proclamation. In the Chinese tradition, the heart receives the mandate of a life. The mandate of the heart to connect the Three Realms. It is a human job then to connect the workings of both heaven and earth to one another. This is not so much considered destiny in the sense of the term Ming, it is more the function or purpose of a human, within the broader context of Daoist thought.

Heaven

Human

Earth

The role of the Shén is twofold, although in truth, the two are the same. First, the Shén is responsible for the constant reception of raw information (i.e., awareness) and second, the Shén helps to create meaning by facilitating connection to, with, or between all things, by emanating out into the world. In both cases, its drive, or "goal" is coherence. It has the role of tying together all three of the realms.

Within the human being, the Shén is the spirit which is most im-

mediately attached to, and most intimately entangled with the workings of the heart-as-organ (Xīn) and the heart-as-mind, or Heart-mind
(also glossed as Xīn). The Shén, as the singular spirit of the Xīn lies at
the center of this volume, and is recognized by many other epithets,
and its workings are recognized in allusions to the "Cinnabar Spirit,"
often encountered in the many Daoist alchemies of the body and spirit, the "Red Bird," as the sentinel and guardian of the Southern quadrate of the cosmos, or even as the Emperor of the South, and correlate
to Yandi (Flame Emperor), who commands, albeit gently, every aspect
of the flame of awareness.

This requires a simultaneity of presence, at once in the world and
also *within* a body; this is the stirring of the Shén (神), incarnated as
jīngshén (精神). This is the diaphanous spirit, open, but imbued with
the urgency, refinement, and direction of embodied essence (the jīng
component of the term "jīngshén").

Alongside the Shén of the Heart, one will encounter the Hún and
Pò cloud spirits and the Yì and the Zhì spirits which form the basis for
the qì within the body. Collectively, five spirits are also called Shén
and they use the same character when referring to the group. This
group of five Shén spirits forms the collective basis for how each of us
is formed, as jīngshén inherited from our parents and also as the basis
for how one "unfolds" into the world. These forms of spirit are native
to the human body and should not be interpreted as invasive or harmful in any way, unless they begin to reach states of disharmony. In this
case, much like an autoimmune condition, the spirits may begin to
act out in a manner unconducive to the health of the whole organism.

Even for all this talk of spirits, this text is not meant to be a magical one. It is meant to be the practice one undertakes so that the
ground from which magic springs is tilled deeply and fertilized. This
is the work in which the valley spirit *begins* to be exhumed from its
deep recesses and hidden coves.

The Trouble with "Qì"

The concept of qì is one of the most ubiquitous ideas to be found
in the Chinese tradition from ancient times to the present day. It is

also one of the most heavily laden terms in the Chinese language, and the sheer weight of its innumerable translations belies its ephemeral nature.

In modern use, the term "qì" (氣) is most often translated as:

- Gas
- Air
- Smell
- Weather
- To make angry
- To annoy
- To get angry
- *Vital energy*

The term *qì* can be used to describe or refer to any number of concepts or events whether interiorized or exteriorized. It is used to describe the functional medium of phenomena and the phenomena themselves, as with the occurrence of weather or with the "force" of emotions. Even the force of one's personality or character finds a place here, in the term *rénqì* (人氣). It is this phrase that points to the change one can make in the world, if the virtues are properly enacted.

Classically, the character for qì (氣) depicted the steam rising from a cooking pot. It was vaporous and subtly tangible if one would only but pay attention. It was also used early on to denote the functioning or work of a thing ("Heart qì" is the beating of the heart to pump blood, for example).

Although it is not considered a classical gloss on the term, one can, understand qì to mean "energy" in the way that prana or pneuma are equated with the loose definition of "energy" within some discussions of the subtle human body in ancient Vedic or Greek traditions as well as the manifold practices that have become tied to these terms. It is acknowledged that this inclusion is, to some extent, forcing the term "qì" to fit contemporary contexts that are not expressly encountered within ancient and classical eras of Chinese culture. With this in mind, the gloss of "energy" will be retained here, as it does persist in many contemporary discussions of qì and is therefore of some value to many persons not versed in the classical associations, as it provide a shorthand for those who may not have exposure to or command of the classical Chinese milieu.

Yin and Yang

The terms Yin and Yang are close relatives of the term qì, and in fact might be considered "templates" of qì. Originally Yin and Yang were represented pictographically on oracular inscriptions as early as the fourteenth century BCE. Visually, Yang was depicted as the bright side of a mound or embankment lit by the sun while Yin was shown as the shaded side of the same.

In use, Yin is a form of potential, being, event, or function which is relatively:

- Female
- Night/Dark/Shaded
- Moist
- Water
- Cold
- Winter
- Death
- Contraction
- Solid

In a contrasted manner, Yang is a form of potential, being, event, or function which is relatively:

- Male
- Day/Light/Brightness
- Dry
- Fire
- Heat
- Summer
- Birth

- Expansion
- Hollow

The terms Yin and Yang are only relative to one another. Absolute forms of either do not exist except as conceptual markers. As such, there is always a more Yin or Yang point of reference in any situation, and the two must be in contact with one another in order for meaning to take place, particularly with respect to a lived body. It is the interplay of Yin and Yang that makes life possible.

The Meaning of Embodiment

From the Daoist perspective, embodiment is an essential part of being in the world. It is not a form to be sloughed off as much as it is meant to be a vehicle for refinement.

The approach taken in this text is such that one can with reality interact at any level as long as it is approached through direct experience. This allows for representation and symbolism to play a direct role in embodiment, just as much as the direct physicality of the body, and much of the work contained in this text will ask the reader to accept the reality of and interact with parts of oneself which may have little or no external "reality" but which are still meaningful to the individual, such as ideas of "benevolence" or "justice."

Many texts will present an idea or theory with little concern for praxis (practice). This is not enough. The idea of Human-ness (rén, 人) is fine in the abstract. For it to be meaningful, though, it must be done. Herein lies one of the potential "difficulties" with this text—that for one to be human, one must live in an embodied space, and that one should "act" in light of this. To read a text will only get one so far—human-ness requires participation through embodiment.

Embodiment can come in many forms and has been ritualized to various extents throughout history, and indeed the performance of ritual can be seen as a transmutation of the ritual from abstract idea to concretized event. This is true at a social level of ritual as well, and our own inner landscapes often mirrored the socio-political landscapes seen in society. This approach is part of what gives texts like the *Daodejing* and the *Huainanzi* their overtly political "flavor." We, as bodies and beings could constitute parts of the body-politic. The cultivation of one as an act of embodiment could therefore help cultivate the many. This is the role of the jūnzǐ (君子), or person of noble character and comportment, an image encountered throughout the text. The jūnzǐ is one for whom the Shen exist an ordinating principles and as co-creators of a life lived with awareness and coherence. In the present text, the reader will encounter themes which can be interpreted as "political," but the reader would do well to consider how any of the themes encountered below apply to the unfolding of a life and how one might act with awareness and coherence both as an individual and as a thriving member of any groups to which one might belong.

The Wǔxíng

The Wǔxíng, or "Five Phase"[3] system of correspondences underpins much of Asian culture, both contemporary and classical. In most iterations, the phases are connected by two main cycles of relation—the growth or generating cycle, and the constricting, or restraining cycle. Given these connections, each of the phases are connected with every other phase.

This system, like that of Yin and Yang mentioned above, can accommodate the categorization of reality based on the similarities that an idea or thing has with one or more of the phases.

The progression of the five phases in the Sheng (growth) cycle is as follows:

- Wood engenders or promotes Fire
- Fire engenders or promotes Earth
- Earth engenders or promotes Metal

3 Also called the "five-element" system in many sources. In some cases, the five elements are viewed as distinct forms or wavelengths of energy that can be manipulated directly. This is consistent with a more occult reading of the Wǔxíng. In this text, however, the phases are used to represent groups of function or quality inherent in existence rather than as distinct and separate forces subject to human operation.

- Metal engenders or promotes Water
- Water engenders or promotes Wood

The progression of the five phases In the Ke (restraining) cycle is as follows:

- Wood restrains Earth
- Earth restrains Water
- Water restrains Fire
- Fire restrains Metal
- Metal restraints Wood

These two cycles will play into nearly every aspect of life according to the five phase dynamics. They will be seen in the interplay of psychological and spiritual phenomena, bodily process, and even distinct modes of human behavior. A familiarity with these two cycles will benefit the reader greatly as they move through the text and as they move through life.

Virtue as Guidepost, Virtue as Goal

For the purposes of this text, the term of virtue has two broad meanings. First, it indicates a quality or behavior which is valued by society, such as trustworthiness, honesty, or steadfastness. Second, can be used to indicate a quality, power, capacity, attribute, or potential of a being. There are times when virtue provides the framework for proper behavior, that is, how one should behave. There are also times when virtue represents the capacity to behave in a certain way. In the reading given here, virtue is not only considered right behavior as determined by a social context, but also the means toward changing oneself toward or away from a quality or capacity. Virtue is, after all, only an expression of qì.

Within the greater Chinese tradition, the importance of, or perhaps one can even go so far as to say the essentiality of virtue for human life in society has been one of the prominent recurring themes regardless of one's philosophical underpinnings.

The Confucian Virtues are parameters for life among other humans. The virtues become both the goal and the method of one's socialized life. The five main Confucian virtues are:

- Rén (仁), the virtue of benevolence, charity, and treating others in a humane fashion. Recognition of the intrinsic human value.
- Yì (義|义), the quality of honesty and uprightness; doing one's best, conscientiousness; steadiness and fairness in action toward others.
- Zhì (智), the wise application of knowledge
- Xìn (信), the virtue of faithfulness and integrity
- Lǐ (禮|礼), correct behavior, or propriety. Can be ritual protocol. Can be etiquette.

The Daoist view of "virtues" are closer to expressions of being-in-itself, rather than as ideals of human behaviour, they are virtues of capacity or power toward oneself *and* others. These virtues do not expressly exist as specific facets of Daoist practice. Instead, they exist as the outcome of good practice and cultivation.

- Ease and Openness of Attitude and Comportment
- Freedom of movement
- Clarity
- Rootedness
- The recognition and embrace of change or flux

By their nature though, even though they are not prescriptive, these attributes are still aspirational in the truest form. The Daoist will still work toward these qualities without having a particular sense of doing, but will strive to achieve these qualities.

It should be noted that, from a Daoist perspective, none of these outcomes are exclusive to the human form, it is merely that humans "know" naturally what to do with openness, clarity, change, and the other Daoist virtues. It is in this way that the virtues assure that the inner human nature of each of us is realized and that Heaven and Earth can be connected.

To say that there is no overlap between Daoist and Confucian virtues, or even to delineate lines of opposition is a nonstarter, at least from the philosophical currents of Daoism inherited from Zhuangzi and Laozi.

One might rightly argue that vast swaths of the Chinese tradition have been undercut in this text as we repeatedly return to Daoist, Confucianist, and Buddhist ideas, and even within these one will find that some technical aspects may go unaddressed. This brevity is purposeful and is meant to render the text more accessible to readers at all levels of experience and understanding. All readers are encouraged to conduct a deeper examination of any and all of the currents mentioned here, and indeed, any others which they might encounter within the broader Chinese tradition. These traditions each have their own viewpoints of, customs around and discussions of Yin, Yang, Shén, ghosts and spirits, proper "stance" in the world, and the like which, in many cases are quite similar. The material represented here is a distillation of work undertaken within aspects of these traditions, and is not intended to represent any of these traditions in totality.

The theme of the Heart is perhaps the most salient commonality that these traditions share, and the Daoist, Confucian, and Buddhist traditions each possess some conception of the Xīn, as the Heart-mind as the locus the operative process of both life and virtue. The Xīn as Heart-mind, in its turn, is collected and enthroned within heart-organ and serves as a mediator of materialized coherence. For the Shén sprits, too, coherence is the key, and further still, working with the Shén spirits is one of the keys to the coherence of the human being.

Do not lose yourself in the philosophy of it. Use the ideas they represent and the qì that each Shen spirit possesses in order to more fully incorporate your own movement as a being on the Human Path.

It is hoped that this text will provide a starting point, a point of initial awareness which the Shén so centrally represents, to other sets of knowledge, and that if one wishes to, that they may use this as a springboard to explore further into the depths of the Chinese tradition and the human condition alike.

Human-ness and Humaneness

What makes one human?

There is, inherent in the two great religious currents native to China, Daoism and Confucianism, the recognition that each human possesses an inner nature and an outer form which help to identify each of us as "human."

What is it though about this human condition which causes us to want to be or to act a certain way? The short answer is that it is just in our nature to do so. To have a certain nature (xìng; 性) is to have certain intrinsic patterns represented. For humanity, there is naturally a "human nature" (rénxìng; 人性), which determines, to some extent, the inherent capacities for and drives toward interaction and togetherness which mark so much of human experience

The *Daodejing* tells us that one should behave with benevolence, toward one's fellow beings, it tells us that one should act from a place of humane behavior. This standard of behavior is such that it allows one room to accept change and to exhibit equanimity while allowing others the same freedom. The *Daodejing* is after all considered a political treatise by many as well as a manual of cultivation. It is only the Dao which views us as "straw dogs," impermanent effigies of little inherent value, save except for sacrifice.

In the Confucianist worldview, the human ought to act in accordance with society by enacting five cardinal virtues which underpin the human experience.

Both of these are unscored by an inner "human" nature (rénxìng; 人性) and a "human" form (rénxíng; 人形).[4]

We will return to the role of humanness within the Daoist metaphysics—as a bridge between Heaven and Earth—throughout the book, but, to begin, what are "heaven" and "earth" in the greater human scheme, according to Chinese custom?

JOHN ANDERSON

---

4 I conceptualize the idea of the human form here to be like the probability functions within the electron shells of atoms...there may be the likelihood a pattern of human form represented as a body, but no one knows what that "actually" is like until it is observed.

Heaven and Earth

One of the repeated themes throughout classical Chinese culture, starting with the Zhou dynasty is the centrality of humankind in the interaction between Heaven and Earth. These two concepts are ubiquitous, and are commonly encountered even within relatively modern settings, but further explication may be helpful to give some of the passages which follow much needed context so as to avoid misconstruing the themes presented in the passages themselves.

The *Yijing*[5] *(易經)* or *Classic of Changes* stands as one of the oldest works of divination in the history of the Chinese civilization. It is a multilayered work whose underpinning philosophy rests on the interplay between Yin and Yang. The first two hexagrams of the system can and can't (Heaven and Earth, respectively) form the basis for all of the other hexagrams to be found in the system. These two principles of Heaven and Earth are both complementary to and necessary for one another within this technique, and this is no less true in the present text. Heaven and Earth must conform to one another.

Heaven as a core concept of Chinese culture is not quite the same as the Judeo-Christian idea of an afterlife in the clouds, marked with pearly gates and golden trumpets. Heaven, or Tiān (天) includes cosmic geography with within it, but Tiān as a force in Chinese culture very often more properly translates to "divinity" or "divine" rather than being attributed to a specific deity-space.[6] In this sense, it is both immanent and impersonal until the person begins to work with

---

5   The term *I Ching* is used as an alternate spelling for this system of divination. Both are correct. The term used in the main body of the text conforms to the convention of modernized pinyin. The term reference here is an older rendering based on the Wade-Giles system of romanization. The term Zhōuyì (周易) is also used in older contexts to indicate this system of divination.

6   Earlier dynasties had a "high God," in the form of Shangti or Shangdi who was represented in an anthropomorphized form, but we do not encounter with Shangdi the sweeping decrees and iron-clad Mandate of Heaven that would be ushered in during the Zhou dynasty. Instead rites performed by the living focused on currying the favor of Shangdi through the intercession of the spirits of one's ancestors or in applying to their power directly. This later idea of "Heaven" and Its Mandate, used to provide dynastic legitimacy or to seed calls for regime change, becomes more formalized and codified during this time, and "Heaven" begins to take on the busy, bureaucratic form that persisted during the following millennia, even as it was left with a line of celestial emperors rather than one Supreme deity to which one prayed.

it. When a human is not in connection with it, Tiān more closely re-sembles a force to be reckoned with, rather than space to be captured or earned. It is only once a person begins the process of connection with the divine that it becomes a space of its own. Here then, one can see Tiān as both lofty and as incarnated.

In contrast to the openness and lightness of heaven, or Tiān, one can see the relative heaviness of Earth as a cosmological principle and counterpoint to heaven. Earth (Kūn; 坤) is a measure of physical-ized space and, when all is balanced, it is a potentiated matrix which allows reality to come forth, but in order for its fecundity to shine through, groundwork must be laid and cultivation must happen to set the scene for any change which is to take place. The soil must be prepared before crops can arise.

Earlier, it was mentioned that Heaven and Earth must conform to one another. This is done through the work of humanity, whose job it is to live the heavenly essence which each of us has been imbued with while preparing the fertile the soils of the self so that the five Shén can shine through in their appropriate manifestations.

Neither Heaven or Earth are considered supernatural in them-selves, they are principles which must be enacted in order for them to have relevance. In addition, neither Heaven nor Earth would be considered pure metaphor. In this way, one must learn to see both metaphor and action, or agency, simultaneously.

It is this capacity within humans which allows us to bridge the cosmic realms of Heaven and Earth.

*   *   *

As you read through the book, you may notice that it does not im-mediately conform to a particular convention of speech, or even of organization. This is purposeful. Classical works can be useful if you are versed in their deeper structure and meaning. Contemporary lan-guage can be useful if you are able to translate many of the older con-cepts represented here. Not every reader will have the tools to do this, and therefore a balance must be reached. An effort has been made to render pertinent ideas accessible while still providing depth to the subject matter.

Fear not, though, you won't be alone in your journey. You will have the company of two old souls: Baby's Breath and Brittle Bones. Sometimes they'll fit on one shoulder, sometimes on the other. Still at other times, you'll have one on either. And yet again, they both might just abscond. Best of luck to you.

Structure of the Passages

Each of the passages in this text are arranged in a similar fashion. Your two companions throughout this guidebook will give you a short dialogue which hits at the heart of the passage. They are wont to present diverging lines on the same thread of thought. The reader would do well to consider these, taken with a grain of salt, perhaps, or reject them altogether. It matters not to those two. And if you are thinking about what is there, deeply engaging it, they will be content anyway.

Following these short vignettes, the reader will find commentary which seeks to address some of the major points of concern and even contention around the subject matter at hand. An effort has been made to avoid heavy use of technical jargon, except where it adds to the conversation, as it tends to confound the reader unduly. Here too, the reader is fully advised to give contemplation to what is said, even if "agreement" is not forthcoming.

Once this commentary has been put in place, the reader is asked to participate in some act, some form of embodiment, some form of doing, which, it is hoped, will root the person in the present, and call out their spirits at the same time. In general, the language in the sections is straightforward, with the exception of the sections containing herbal practice. In these sections, it should be borne in mind that any herbal formula mentioned here can be taken internally, but what is truly important in the context of the passage is the ruling principle of the formula. For example, if the overall structure of the formula indicates that it helps to "calm the mind" by regulating the heartbeat, based on its ingredients, the goal is to regulate the heartbeat. In these cases, the formulas serve as both signpost and praxis. The material in this section is meant to be undertaken. It is meant to be done. Given these practices, it is hoped that this book should better fill the role of workbook than textbook.

Lastly in each of the passages, the reader will find secondary commentary on the role that the ideas contained in the passage can play in a wider worldview. That is, how the material helps one to be more humane toward others.

In short, the practices here are meant to be embodied, and they are meant to be engaged. The structure of the passage first provides a sense of being to oneself, through physical movement, through contemplation, through directed internal dialogue, through mindfulness and awareness of what is *as well as* being unto others, being for others as well as being for oneself. The two are not mutually exclusive.

One can be both magnanimous and sagacious, as the jūnzǐ (君子) and the shèngrén (聖人) can embrace one another.

Technical Considerations

This book is not intended to be a "purist" work, and should not be construed as such. This is true of its general outlook and philosophy, as well as the style and source of translation. Any discrepancy in definition and any ambiguity in concept is solely due to the choices made in the writing this text, and are mine alone.

Textual Choice

It will be abundantly clear to many readers that the text takes a somewhat medicalized approach to the Shén. That is to say, much of the correspondence structure of the wuxing (i.e., "Five Phase") system is drawn from Chinese medicine as a discipline. There are two things which need to be considered here, though. First, the goal is not to reduce the Shén to the five phases or vice versa. There is rich context that each can add to the other, regardless of where the information is drawn from. The work shown herein is individual, and each will add their own idiosyncrasies to the process.

As a practical choice, much of the medical literature provides one of the fullest arrangements of the five phase correspondences, and the subject matter is, at least on some level, accessible to most readers. If, by contrast, a strictly "magical" approach to the correspondences had been taken, it would very quickly have alienated a great number of readers who might otherwise gain something from the commentary and praxis. At the same time, it should be reinforced that a concerted effort has been made to steer away from extremely technical aspects of Ru-Mo (Confucianist) and Daoist philosophies. Neither of these is monolithic and the reader is encouraged to explore the subjects more fully at their leisure.

Pinyin/Wade-Giles

The pinyin style of romanization has been adopted throughout the book. The Wade-Giles system is still in use, but it represents an older approach that has largely fallen out of favor with students, authors, and teachers of classical and contemporary Chinese language and culture.

Every reasonable effort has been made to provide the pinyin and the character for relevant foreign terms. As a general rule, the traditional characters have been chosen when referring to Chinese terms. This was a personal choice, and should not be taken as a categorical endorsement nor should it constitute a statement of legitimacy. Again, it was a choice.

*   *   *

It is truly my hope that this text provides a starting point for the reader—an opening to a more Human path. This path will look different for each of us, but it should be led by the Shén spirit we all naturally possess.

This text is not intended to be a work of magic or alchemy in a strict reading of these terms. It is, however, part of the work which must be undertaken and maintained before one engages with more esoteric practices.

Transmutation is important, and perhaps in this sense, there is yet alchemy to be done and magic to be had.

With this in mind—listen, open, and become gently pliable as you read ahead.

Find your virtue and power and take that Way.

稚子气概：

做一個有朝氣的人就是保護陽，因為陽是生命的
力量。

Zhìzǐ Qìgài:

Zuò yīgè yǒu zhāoqì de rén jiùshì bǎohù yáng, yīnwèi yáng shì shēngmìng de lìliàng.

脆骨：

它是火與水，僅此而已

Cuìgú:

Tā shì huǒ yǔ shuǐ, jǐn cǐ éryǐ.

Preserving the Yang

"Baby's Breath":

To be a vibrant human is to protect the Yang, for the Yang is the force of one's life.

It is the spark of movement which simultaneously impels and signifies life.

To know the Yang is to know the Red Bird which alights from the South.[7]

"Brittle Bones":

If you want to know how the Yang is stored and protected, you must know the Yin as well.

It is fire and water, and nothing more.

Consult the *Yijing*! The Classic of Permutations sees the interplay of fire and water in the body in this way:

Deep under the ocean it is an alien place for us. This is the utmost Yin. We humans cannot live there, and cannot directly experience it, but there is life which flourishes there.

---

7 The four cardinal directions of the cosmos are held in place and protected by the Four Animals, which are the concretized forms of the qualities of the direction. The Southern quadrate is guarded by the "Red Bird," the Western quadrate is secured by the "White Tiger," the Northern quadrate is overseen by the "Black Tortoise," and the Eastern quadrate is presided over by the "Green Dragon."

Even in the most Yin place there is the spark of Yang. There are deep fires which will never come to surface.

Within the body, this is the dark, hidden space between the kidneys—the Mingmen (命門), or "Gate of Life."[8] The emergence of the Shén from the darkness at the center of the Mingmen is the same as when the volcano finally breaks the surface of the ocean to fulfill its destiny (Ming) providing the volatility, power, and raw substance needed to build new land.

This is the manifestation of Yin as an accumulated substance (new yin). It is the upwelling which surpasses the great Yin of the ocean. This is the 64th image in the Book of Permutations.[9]

Then and only then can things be built in a way that we can use them!

The Yang gives life to Yin.

"Baby's Breath":

Even still, once this happens you have not quite reached the White Gate. One still resides in the darkness.

This is an upwelling of the spirit which occurs not only once life emerges and there is consciousness, but when one is able to project itself into the world.

---

8   Mingmen is also translated as "Gate of Destiny." This is somewhat in line with the idea of passing or transmitting information down through generations. That is, within Daoist cosmology, we receive an allotted "destiny" or capacity for experience, from Heaven, which is then "filtered" through the energy and experience contributed by both parents.

9   I.e., the Yijing. The premise of the Yijing rests upon the casting of line sets which give images of divinatory import, and which in turn can evolve and change, and within which constituent lines also present unfolding possibilities or contexts within a situation.

This is the valley spirit arising from the Gorge! The valley spirit is rooted by the Mud Ball. This is the Yang properly rooted deep within the upper Yin, but which can then move as it needs to.

Freed from the utmost constraints of the Yin, and into the Yang aspects of the universe wherein many of the spirits dwell. This is the first opening of the eyes. This is the emergent Hún.

Just as Taibai heralds the coming of Ruo in the sky, so does the arising of the Hún presage the emergence of the Shén.

Yin heralds Yang!

"Brittle Bones":

The earth moves upward, towards the Sun. Even at great heights such as those that mountains can reach, laboriously, slowly, the Yang of the Winds will pare it down.

This is the 53rd image in the *Yijing*.

The gradual progress of rising to a great height after a very long and arduous process of steady accumulation.

It will be worn down, even as it rises!

In the same manner, the Shén and Hún[10] as Yang can carry Yin, but only so far. Eventually the Yin will be ground down or consumed. The Yin must then submerge in order to rise up once more.

To protect the Yang is to move it only when movement is called for and to keep it at rest when stillness is necessary.

10 The *Huangdi Neijing Lingshu* says that the Hún spirit is the "coming and going" of the Shén. It is part of the Hún's charge to provide the Shén with this capacity, while the Shén provides consciousness of the process.

COMMENTARY

THE YANG IS an ever-emergent active process which must be promoted and safe-guarded, as it is the base energy of life. It is the deepest fire which is necessary to heat the Sānjiāo (三焦), or "Triple Burners" which are likened to the furnaces of the human body.

To be alive, to experience Life, there must be warmth, movement, and expansion. When the Yang invigorates the Shén and this in turn is properly rooted in the Upper Yin, or "Sea of Marrow" then one can proceed to move clearly and easily within the world.

By its nature, Yang is volatile and will move and ascend, but it cannot be left to fly away. The Yang must needs be anchored, contained, and, at least to some extent, directed if it is to be of any sustained use to the individual. It must be housed, contained, and nourished in a manner that allows both restraint and movement, and which facilitates both the root and the flowering of the Yang, depending on the needs of the situation.

This is the role of the Yin.

To move, to grow, and to evolve, the Function that is the Yang must be contained in the Form that is the Yin. In addition, there is a fundamental paradox with regard to the preservation and transformation of Yang and Yin as a unified pair. In order for Yang to be preserved there must be stillness. This much is somewhat intuitive. There must also be sufficient movement to facilitate the conservation of Yang. There are mythological accounts[11] involving the origins of the Manchu people in China which illustrate the same transformation and rooting of the active potential of Yang: "The Manchu ancestors were born by a pool after a goddess, by mistake, ate a plant seed held in the beak of a red bird."[12]

J O H N   A N D E R S O N

11 Wei Haiquan, Hiromitsu Taniguchi, and Liu Ruoxin, "Chinese Myths and Legends for Tianchi Volcano Eruptions," *Northeast Asian Studies* 6 (2002): 191–200.

12 As a figure, the Red Bird is associated with both fire and creation in Chinese culture, and also has some of the characteristics of the phoenix birds found throughout many other world mythologies.

We see in this short vignette the quickening of Yin principle (the seed) by being held within the Yang principle, (the beak of the Red Bird). The enlivened seed subsequently becomes contained within the body of the goddess as it is ingested, gestated, and born into life once again.

The Yang of the body must be preserved precisely because it is this which gives the first power and germination to form and allows for the transformation of the same.

There is another form of Yang which cuts to the heart directly, particularly within the Confucian, Buddhist, and Mohist lines of thought which are presented within this text.[13] This is the broad concept of "virtues" as they are found within the Chinese culture. In the *Baihu Tongde Lun* (白虎通德論), virtue, or dé (德), pertains to the Yang, while the emotions (qíng; 情) pertain to the Yin, and either of these can be used to reinforce Yang or Yin, respectively.[14]

Virtues exist as attributes, as ideals of behavior, as well as means for cultivation of qì. Each of these can affect the unfolding of one's life and how one reacts to one's destiny, or Mìng (命).[15]

To preserve and grow the Yang (yǎngshēng; 養生) is to practice virtue, and to practice virtue is to preserve and nurture the Yang.

13 It cannot be emphasized enough that Daoist, Buddhist, and Confucian ideas, philosophies, and practices all borrowed from one another throughout Chinese history. Daoism in particular stands as an example of a syncretic process in which there are many "versions" of Daoism (Zhengyi, Lingbao, and and Maoshan are but three lines of Daoist religion and practice, which represent both orthodox and heterodox currents). Each of these schools contribute something to the greater corpus of Daoist knowledge. The same process can be applied to Buddhism as a whole, and Confucianism as well. As such, it would be a mistake to assume that any of these three currents (i.e., Daoism, Buddhism, and Confucianism) found within the Chinese tradition are monolithic or static.

14 Heiner Fruehauf (trans.) "On Humanity's Emotions and Higher Virtues: A Passage from the Chapter "Qingxing" in the *Baihu tongde lun* (*Discussions on the Power of Virtue in the White Tiger Hall*; attributed to Ban Gu) fl. 1st Century CE," 2015: https://classicalchinesemedicine. org/humanitys-emotions-higher-virtues-passage-chapter-qingxing-baihu-tongde-lun-discussions-power-virtue-white-tiger-hall-ban-gu/ [Last accessed 26 Nov 2020].

15 The concept of Ming (命), or "destiny" as it exists in the Chinese culture is complex and, for Western readers, often very confusing. Modern translations include "life," as in a life path, "fate," "an order or command," or "to be assigned a name or title." Each of these is said to take place at birth and are said to color the course of one's life, although one's Mìng (命) does not determine a person's life course as such. The many definitions of this term reflect the ambivalence that is found within Chinese culture toward ideas of fate and determinism. On the one hand, it is desirable to see one's own way, but it is also laudable to uphold the destiny which one receives from Heaven.

The Embodiment

The principles of Yin and Yang are relative as concepts and can be abstracted in all sorts of ways, but in the human body it is all of the principles of lightness, motion, and heat. The Yang of the human body allows for movement and growth, transformation and interpenetration. It is a pool of potential from which we draw when we choose to act within the world. It is the force of our own agency, and it is finite. We can, however, make sure that the Yang is drawn down in a slower and much more controlled fashion.

This ability to conserve the Yang is vital to the vibrant functioning of the body, as once Yang becomes firmly depleted, inertia begins to slow, and the body begins to grow colder and heavier.

The Yang affects more than the physical function of the body. More subtle structures within the human experience also find their animus within the Yang. For example, the Yang of the Heart energizes the Shén and the other indwelling spirits, while blood which is properly infused with the force and the fire of the Yang helps to move the spirits and consequently allows them the power to interact with the external world.

More mundane, though equally subtle, facets of the human experience are likewise informed by the state of the Yang. Motivation and the desire to interact with others is very contingent on the state of the Yang, given that it provides the capacity for one to extend oneself into the world, and into hypothetical futures.

There are several avenues to pursue in the preservation of one's Yang. They can be boiled down to the following:

- Food/Herbs
- Action/Inaction (consider the timing of the seasons)
- Energetic Practices (qigong, breathwork, virtue work, prayer/contemplation, etc.)

Each of these are components of a group of practices which form a tradition known in Chinese as yǎngshēng (养生)which is most often translated as "Nourishing of Life" and which provides broad guidelines of conduct in order to assure that a person is able to live life to its longest, fullest extent and which at the same time is said to give depth to an unfolding life. This is because this tradition encourages awareness of the body and of the spirit as well as fostering an understanding of how one ought to interact with the world.

To be clear, there is no single way to protect and preserve the Yang, and each of the broad categories above deserve greater elucidation. This is precisely because it may ultimately take several techniques to safeguard the Yang of the body.

Preservation of the Yang with Food and Herbs

To most, it may seem somewhat underwhelming that one's choice in food can help foster or preserve the deepest life forces of an individual. So much emphasis is placed on more esoteric aspects of cultivation praxis that more mundane topics very often end up unnoticed or deemphasized. However, the proper use of food and foodways is one of the easiest and most accessible ways of maintaining and preserving health (another translation for the term yǎngshēng).

So, what does it mean to preserve one's Yang with food?

It is tempting to seize immediately upon the nature of Yang as a guideline. By its nature, Yang is relatively hot in nature, while Yin by way of contrast is relatively cold. It is therefore intuitive to think of taking in hot-natured, moving, or volatile foods or foods which are served hot as a means to preserve Yang. It should be sufficient to eat hot peppers, dried ginger, cinnamon, and mutton, or to take fuzi (aconite) or shujiao (xanthoxylum) based decoctions.[16] Alas, this is somewhat akin to putting gasoline on a small campfire. It will burn very hot for a short period, but afterward the fire will not be able to maintain itself as the fuel is expended too quickly and burns too intensely to be maintained. This approach is very much the opposite of preserving the Yang.

If Yin provides the ground, the weight, and the gravity which

---

16 Both are generally considered "hot" in nature, and thus may be of use when the yang is severely depleted, but they will do precious little good if taken only on their own. They need to be used in the context of a complete and balanced meal or formula.

keeps the Yang from dissipating due to its own expansive nature, it would also be intuitive to emphasize heavier, denser, foods. This, too, is tricky in terms of sustained conservation. In addition to being dense and heavy, foods considered to be Yin also tend to be cold-natured, viscous, and cloying. In effect, this would amount to putting out the fire of the body.

The Yang needs a base from which to grow and radiate—it must be moored in such a way that it can move, but not float away. It also needs a space within which it is contained. As much as the Yang tends to expand, it must have boundaries. This is the purview of the Yin, and the two must work in concert.

According to Chinese medical tradition, diet is an integral and necessary component of this endeavor. Yang strengthening and preserving foods include the following:

- Grains: quinoa, sweet (glutinous) rice, wheat germ
- Vegetables: leek, mustard greens, onion, radish, scallion, squash, sweet potato, turnip, watercress
- Fruit: cherry, litchi, logan (berry), peach, raspberry, strawberry
- Nuts and seeds: chestnuts, pinenuts, pistachio nuts, walnuts
- Fish: anchovy, lobster, mussel, prawn, shrimp, trout
- Meat: chicken, lamb, venison, kidneys (both beef and lamb)

The cooking method can affect this as well, with methods such as roasting and baking being more amenable to preserving Yang, while raw and steamed foods can contribute less to the process (or even inhibit it, in the case of prolonged ingestion of raw foods).

See the subsequent passage "On Nourishment" in the current work for a fuller treatment of the effects caused by the intake of food, drink, and other substances on the Shén spirit.

Let us now turn our gaze to one herbal formula which does just this and glean what we can from its structure and action.

Qianyang Dan[17] is composed of the following ingredients:

- Fùzǐ (附子) (Aconite)
- Guībǎn (龟板) (Turtle Plastron)
- Shārén (砂仁) (Amomum)
- Zhìgāncǎo (炙甘草) (Prepared Licorice)

Qianyang Dan, or "Submerge the Yang Pill" centers on the containment of Yang in its proper place while allowing it room to roam.

Fùzǐ (aconite) is the herb par excellence for gathering the Yang to its proper placements, namely in the areas between the kidneys and in a different, though no less important manner, in the chest as well.

Guībǎn (turtle plastron) assures the Yang is kept in place by providing the anchoring force of Yin, a function assisted by the Shārén (amomum).

Lastly, Zhìgāncǎo (licorice processed with honey) assures that the interplay between the ingredients is smooth and harmonious and, further, that they do not affect the digestive system.

This simple, yet powerful formula "submerges" the Yang in its lower area of origination (again, roughly in the space between the two kidneys), where it is amassed and subsequently used when the normal mechanism of qì production are overtaxed or otherwise inadequate for the needs of the individual.

By the same token, food, then, that is meant to safeguard the Yang should be an admixture of the two. Hot or warm foods will work to stoke the Yang, while denser foods can assure that the Yang will stay in the system long enough for it to be transformed and used. Under the right circumstances, the Yang within the food can ultimately be stored. The right meal can deeply warm the body, while the wrong meal can cause burning gastric reflux.

To moderate this, bland foods and herbs can be used as the material base of a meal. Many grains fit into this category, and most are said to strengthen the middle jiao (i.e., the digestive system), itself an

17 Heiner Fruehauf, "Qianyang Dan: A Key Formula of the Sichuan Fire School—An In-depth Interview with Heiner Fruehauf" (2009): http://www.classicalchinesemedicine.org/wp-content/uploads/2012/04/fruehauf_qianyangdanENG.pdf [Last accessed 6 Dec 2020].

arbiter of the Yin and the Yang of the body.

In addition to these considerations, be aware of the climate and the calendar. Eat with the present and future seasons in mind. That is, avoid cold foods in the winter, and be wary of the over-consumption of hot foods in the summer.

Movement and Rest in the Safeguarding of the Yang

The previous clause applies not only to the timely and proper intake of food that possesses the appropriate characteristics. It also applies when we are considering how one's Yang is expended. Yang is conserved when we are at rest. Relaxation is key to this, and it is a pursuit engaged by too few of us.

For many of us, the mind never stops. The so-called "monkey mind" chattering and chittering away cannot be quieted easily, and while it may not be as apparent as physical activity, the overexertion of the mind will also expend the Yang.

There is a fundamental paradox here, too. The Yang is a principle of movement, and in order that the Yang is encouraged and conserved, there must be some level of movement when the time is appropriate. Yang must be exercised consistently even if only mildly. Sedentary lifestyles will eventually deplete the Yang through an atrophy of its energetic potential.

Work to stretch the Body, the Mind, the senses, and the Shén gently and learn to retract and quiet these when the work is done. This generally requires an inward-directed observation. The inner focus lies at the root of many of the other techniques outlined in this text, and it directly informs the ideas of cultivation mentioned below.

Energetic Cultivation and the Yang

The idea of cultivation must needs be addressed early in any discussion of any of the applied techniques of Eastern philosophy, such as meditation, qigong, and other more esoteric practices. Each of these requires the participant to foster capacities within him or herself which take repeated practice and refinement. The length of practice performed day-to-day is not of primary importance here, but the consistency of practice is. That is, it is often better to practice for a few minutes each day than it is to practice for an hour every week. The mind and the body accept the rhythm of the practice much more readily when it is applied in this manner. As the practice becomes more ingrained, the effort applied will become easier, and the length of experience will increase.

Many forms of practice can be used to strengthen the Yang. Here we will mention three—two of which are quite esoteric, and the third of which is accomplished much more readily, and by almost anyone. The first of the three provides the easiest entry to the subject at hand—sun-bathing. The next two—"thunder-breathing" and spinal circulation—require greater awareness overall and a more nuanced, and somewhat more esoteric, view of the mind and body. Let us begin with the most elementary and most accessible technique mentioned here.

Sunbathing

All that is required for this activity is that one go outdoors and sit in the sun. In this exercise, the goal is to absorb the Yang of the Sun through the skin in a mindful fashion.[18]

18 The same practice can be used to absorb Yin from the Lunar body. A more esoteric form of this practice is found in Maspero: "To absorb solar energy, at dawn when the Sun first rises, sit or stand up, concentrate your attention, and click your teeth nine times. Then from the bottom of your heart, invoke the essence of the Sun which shines like a pearl with green reflection and visualize it changing into a red halo, bright and mysteriously flamboyant. Next, close your eyes, hold them tightly shut, and visualize the five colors of the Sun spreading into a halo and coming to touch your body. Allow them to sink as far down as the feet and reach as high up as the top of the head. Next, see the center of the brilliant cloud in a purple hue like the pupil of an eye. Repeat this process ten times. Then join the five colors together and let them enter your mouth to swallow them. Do this swallowing of solar energy forty-five times, then swallow the saliva nine times and clap the teeth nine times. (2.19a; Henri Maspero, *Taoism and Chinese Religion*, tr. by Frank A. Kierman Jr., [Amherst: University of Massachusetts Press, 1981], 514); Tao Hongjing gives another form of the same exercise: "To absorb solar energies, write the character for 'Sun' in a square or circle nine inches in size, using vermilion ink on green paper. Every morning, turn east, hold the paper in the left hand, and concentrate on it until it turns into the resplendent Sun itself. Then swallow it and let it remain in your heart; click the teeth nine times and swallow saliva nine times. You may also add the absorption of Sun rays to your practice. Do this three times a day, facing east in the morning, south at noon, and west in the afternoon. Visualize a red sun with a bright red radiance as big as a large coin in your heart, then allow its nine rays to rise from the heart into the throat and let them reach

Sit in a comfortable position and allow the heat to infuse the skin with warmth. You may feel an effusive flush over the skin as the blood begins to circulate into relaxed capillaries.

Limit your exposure so as to avoid skin damage. Ten minutes is doable on most days, but do not allow much more than 15 minutes in a session. Tanning is not the goal here. Also, avoid this exercise if there is an allergic reaction.

Use your awareness to direct this energy into the lower Dantian, roughly one or two inches below and posterior to the navel. From this space, it is possible to move it into the space between the Kidneys wherein the Primordial Fire is said to reside.

Thunder Breathing

Next is a visualization technique used to treat Gu syndromes, encountered in the early seventh-century text. *Zhubing Yuanhou Lun*.[19] A variant of this practice also provides one of the most perfunctory steps of various techniques to call forth and control thunder as they are still employed within religious Daoism.

In this technique, one sits or preferably lies supine (belly up) in a comfortable, but not overly relaxed manner. He or she closes the eyes and clicks the teeth together until saliva begins to accumulate in the mouth. Each clicking of the teeth should be imagined from the standpoint of a creature that is extremely small. To this entity, the clicking of the teeth would be deafening, and the vibrations caused by this action would reverberate and crash as if peals of thunder are near.

the inside of your teeth. However, do not let them pass beyond the teeth but send them back down into the abdomen. Visualize them distinctly in your heart and belly. Then let them leave together with the breath and swallow the saliva thirty-nine times. (2.14a–16b; Maspero, *Taoism and Chinese Religion*, 514–15).

19 "Find a comfortable position, either sitting up or lying down. Place your internal focus on the abdomen, feeling it expand as you breathe in and collapse as you breathe out. Keep swallowing the saliva that accumulates in your mouth, imagining that it is thunder and lightning that permeate every corner of the abdomen. Gu is a yin pathogen, hidden and stagnant, and it takes a constant inundation with yang energy to drive it out. Thunder and lightning represent the most yang phenomena in nature." From Heiner Fruehauf, "Driving Out Demons and Snakes—Gu Syndromes: A Forgotten Clinical Approach to Chronic Parasitism," 11: https://classicalchinesemedicine.org/wp-content/uploads/2015/10/fruehauf_drivingout.pdf [Last accessed 26 Nov 2020].

Allow this qì to resound and diffuse throughout the jaws and head.

The mind should be coordinated with the working of the jaw so that you visualize or "see" a flash each time the teeth strike together. This is rarely like seeing a single bolt of lightning and more like the illumination occuring in an area when lightning occurs behind us so that the light provides an all-encompassing strobe effect.

In this way, the Yang nature of bright light and sudden, loud sounds infuse the saliva[20] held in the mouth. This is then swallowed with vigor and is carried down to the stomach to energize the Middle Burner. It infuses Yang into every space of the abdomen, no matter how constricted or minute. This, in turn breaks apart the Yin energy embodied by the Gu parasite. In addition, some of this energy can be sent down to the Lower Burner and used in a similar fashion or stored in a manner described in the next exercise.

Spinal Circulation of Yang

The last method mentioned here is ubiquitous, spanning innumerable sources encountered across many traditions. This practice is part of the larger practice of Daoyin, the history of which is dated to at least the fourth century BCE.[21] The earliest evidence for this type of practice is found on a carved block from the Zhou dynasty.

The inscription on the dodecanal block reads:

> To guide the qì, allow it to enter deeply [by inhaling] and collect it [in the mouth]. As it collects, it will expand. Once expanded, it will sink down. When it sinks down, it comes to rest. After it has come to rest, it becomes stable. When the qì is stable, it begins to sprout. From sprouting, it begins to grow. As it grows, it can be pulled back upwards. When it is pulled upwards, it reaches the crown of the head. It then touches above at the crown of the head and below at the base of the spine.

---

20 In many Eastern traditions, the saliva is held to be a highly refined substance and it is therefore capable of receiving and retaining the Yang that accumulates during the exercise.

21 Donald Harper, *Early Chinese Medical Literature: The Mawangdui Medical Manuscripts.* (New York: Kegan Paul, 1998).

Who practices like this will attain long life. Who goes against this will die.[22]

As the name implies the practice seeks to move the Yang up and down the spine, with continued practice resulting in an increasing ease with which the exercise is performed. This is true of any of the exercises laid out in this text.

To begin, sit comfortably, keeping the spine as straight as is natural for you. In the beginning, it may be helpful to use a chair in order to assist the spine in remaining straight. Do not be overly concerned with maintaining perfect spinal posture, but make sure that the spine is as straight as can be sustained.

Become aware of a space below the umbilicus approximately two to three inches and situated behind the umbilicus two to three inches. This is the approximate space of the lowest of the body's three Dantians ("Cinnabar Fields"). This space extends posteriorly from behind the umbilicus to just behind the spine. It is in this area that the most primordial form of Yang (Yuanqi) is contained. In this area, common sensations include a feeling of warmth or an expansive pressure which occur once the area has been accessed and activated via directed awareness and concentration. Even more profound felt-senses may arise here as the person continues to work with the qì in this area.

Once the sustained sensation of warmth has been achieved in the lower Dantian, guide this heat slowly up the spine. Also common is a mild heaviness or pressure moving up the spine, or even a prickling or an itch that travels up the spine as the person concentrates.

Be mindful of any change to this movement of qì: when it stops,[23] when it becomes difficult,[24] when there is a difference in temperature, pain, or other physical changes.

If you are able to bring the Yang qì up to the head, let it reside there for a very short period before letting it "fall" back down the spine like a warm rain.

JOHN ANDERSON

22 Harper, *Early Chinese Medical Literature*, 126.
23 Often indicative of a blockage in the jinglou or "meridians" of the body.
24 Similarly, this indicates that there is a resistance to movement of the qì. If the qì still moves, maintain awareness until the qì is able to move through this space.

44

Relax into this.

In addition, if there is noticeable heat which is being held in the head, neck or shoulders let it be carried back down the spine with the Yang which you have directed.

Let it come to rest in the space below the navel and between the kidneys. This is the proper lodging place of the Yang when it is not in use. Thus one part of life is conserved.

Repeat this exercise for several cycles as you are able. Try as much as possible to devote time every day to this and other Yang preserving practices, even if only for a few minutes. It is better to do this than to spend two hours performing them once a month. There is generally very little growth in this sporadic practice of cultivation.

Perhaps most importantly, this exercise, adapted from broader Daoyin practices serves to put the person into contact with their own embodiment.

> Daoyin serves to increase practitioners' internal awareness of health and enhances their urge for balance and harmony, making it easy and even essential to practice an overall moderation that pervades all aspects of life.[25]

As for the role of virtue (dé; 德) in preservation of Yang, we will revisit this topic, as it is folded into the larger conversation about "spirits" and the role of the collective Shén as components of the human psyche, and emotions as the text unfurls. Know that the state of the Yang is intimately tied to the depth of incarnation, and virtue is but one manifestation of the Yang

To Be Humane

The connection between the state of one's Yang and the ease with which one engages with humaneness and humanity may not be immediately apparent. That is, until you think about how you interact

25 Livia Kohn, *Chinese Healing Exercises: The Tradition of Daoyin* (Honolulu: University of Hawaii Press, 2008), 16.

with others when you are very cold and/or very tired—two of the main physiological symptoms of Yang deficiency. One is even called "cold" when they are unable or unwilling to engage with others. Other psychic sequalæ of Yang deficiency include depression and withdrawal. This amounts to a difficulty in establishing both contact and connection with other beings. The Shén derives much of its ability to interact with other Shén from the Yang, and a deficit in the state of the Yang can deeply impair the capacity for personal interaction.

The person may wish in earnest to initiate, establish, and maintain meaningful relationships with others, but if the Yang is not available, the effort cannot be sustained, if it is initiated at all. Alternately, the Yang deficient person may be unable to ensure the coherence of his or her boundaries within the human interaction, which opens one or both up to an inequality or even an abuse of energetic exchange between the two. This relational boundary is vital to human interaction, although its permutations can vary greatly from encounter to encounter and from culture to culture. The state of the Yang is essential to the ebb and flow of interrelatedness regardless of the cultural expression of it.

稚子气概：

善良对他人有好处，因此他们可以自由移动，成
长和创造。

如果可以避免，请勿对他人造成伤害。

公平不是仁慈。

契合不是仁慈，尽管对某些人来说就是那样。

宽容不一定是善良的.

Zhìzǐ Qìgài:

Shànliáng duì tārén yǒu hǎochù, yīncǐ tāmen kěyǐ zìyóu yídòng, chéngzhǎng hé chuàngzào.

Rúguǒ kěyǐ bìmiǎn, qǐng wù duì tārén zàochéng shānghài.

Gōngpíng bùshì réncí.

Shǒufēngqín bùshì réncí, jǐnguǎn duì mǒu xiē rén lái shuō jiùshì nàyàng.

Kuānróng bù yīdìng shì shànliáng de.

脆骨：

與少數其他人共享的所謂"仁慈"很少與整個世界共享，並且通常只有著眼於認可。

這不是仁慈！

…

這是對自己說的一個愉快的謊言。這肯定在"幽靈之路"上。

Cuìgú:

Yǔ shǎoshù qítā rén gòngxiǎng de suǒwèi "réncí" hěn shǎo yǔ zhěnggè shìjiè gòngxiǎng, bìngqiě tōngcháng zhǐyǒu zhuóyǎn yú rènkě.

Zhè bùshì réncí!

…

Zhè shì duì zìjǐ shuō de yīgè yúkuài de huǎngyán. Zhè kěndìng zài "yōulíng zhī lù" shàng.

On Benevolence

"Baby's Breath":

For better or worse, our being has a gravity.

Our behaviors and affects and countenance all have weight.

If, as the *Daodejing* tells us, we but are straw dogs in the workings of the Dao, then kindness is a thing of the human realm.

Benevolence is doing well unto others so that they may move freely, grow, and create.

Do not work toward the harm of another if it can be avoided.

Fairness is not benevolence.

Accordance is not benevolence, though it can feel that way to some.

Neither is permissiveness necessarily benevolent

The *Daodejing* says:

"In giving, the best thing is being like Heaven."[26]

If you are going to practice benevolence, be invisible.

Let the recipient experience grace by practicing anonymity. This is the wind. It is seen only in relation to the movement of other things,

---

26 R. Henricks, *Te-Tao Ching*, 60.

but it is felt, nonetheless.

Leave the world with more clarity and ease than when you arrived in it!

"Brittle Bones":

As the Madman chants:

"Don't scratch my wandering,
my twisty whimsy wandering,
Don't scratch these carefree feet!"[27]

The so-called "benevolence" that is shared with a select few other people is rarely shared with the world as a whole, and commonly, only with an eye toward recognition.

This is not benevolence!

In the name of Beneficence, shaking so many hands, yet never touching a person.

It is a pleasant lie spoken to oneself. This is surely on the Path of the Ghost.

It does not easily square with the Human Path.

Even as you are benevolent to one, strive to be benevolent to all you encounter.

---

27 David Hinton, (Trans.), *Chuang Tsu—The Inner Chapters* (Berkeley: Counterpoint Press, 2014)

COMMENTARY

BENEVOLENCE IS BY its very nature a stance toward other beings. It needs a subject upon which to work.[28]

At the root of benevolence as an act, there is an evenness in one's comportment toward others as well as an unconditional regard for them and a willingness to act on the behalf of others for the purposes of ease, lack of artifice, expression, and harmony both within oneself and toward others as shown in the 42nd hexagram of the *Yijing*, "Increase" or Yì (益). Here, though, the increase is not of an individual, but of all, receiving benefit from above. As action, one shows benevolence to all who are less capable of cultivation.

To be quietly benevolent is best if one is to follow the Daoist tendancy toward softness and silence, but to say the giver does so for no return or exchange whatsoever is incomplete. It is because benevolence as a virtue practice is a work of cultivation that, as an action, it is neither done in pure anonymity nor as absolute altruism. The commentary on the fifth line of hexagram 42 states:

> The fifth NINE [a yang line], undivided, shows its subject with sincere heart seeking to benefit (all below). There need be no question about it; the result will be great good fortune. (All below) will with sincere heart acknowledge his goodness.[29]

Still, recognition is not the end goal in this instance. Change of being is of utmost importance. As with many forms of cultivation, there is a transmission from one to another. As you are benevolent to others, they too may be benevolent to still others. This is cultivation of a group or area.

28 Although you can practice benevolence toward all beings, this is: 1) still a subject and 2) quite difficult for most of us and therefore usually requires some experience in working with individual beings at the outset.

29 James Legge, (Trans.), *The I Ching*. Sacred Books of the East, vol. 16, (1899). Internet Sacred Text Archive. https://www.sacred-texts.com/ich/ic42.htm [Last accessed on 1 Dec 2020].

In this hexagram, a group of people come together in accordance with each other and with a focus on the larger group and larger projects, under the direction of one who is giving good and upright guidance to the whole. This individual is not the most important part of this dynamic. The benevolence bestowed to others is paramount. As such possessing the quality of right behavior for the betterment of others is an individual manifestation, but its outcome belongs to others.

This is the cultivation of the group through the cultivation of its members. The benevolence of one person to another is the beginning of benevolence from one person to a group and from that group to another group.

In order for larger group efforts to take place, they must begin with the individual benevolence which so often serves as the standard for humane behavior wherein we treat others in a manner such that they will work for our betterment as well as their own, but there is a point of caution for all of this discussion: do not confuse the performance of benevolence and the feelings which it can bring with the acts and words associated with the appearance of benevolence. To be benevolent is to do right by others as one can, not to talk about doing benevolent things. It must, as in all things, come naturally and without major effort.

The Embodiment

The work of benevolent regard is not only a recognition of behaviors which ought to be enacted. It is also a state of mind, of presence which one can cultivate. It is a stance toward other human beings. This is largely the idea behind "compassion" as it is viewed within the corpus of Buddhist practices. In the Daoist read of it, one looks to the jūnzǐ (also, chun tzu; 君子) as an exemplar of "right" behavior, and thus, benevolence. The Ritsema and Karcher translation of the *Yijing* gives the following definition for the term jūnzǐ: "[it is]...the ideal of a person who uses divination to order his/her life in accordance with

[dao] rather than willful intention."[30] That is, he or she acts not from an individual will to do or be, but from a deeper place from whence time and destiny find issuance (i.e., the Dao).

This may be an accurate start within a discussion on the importance and role of divination in ancient societies, but perhaps additional context is necessary in order to unpack the term more completely. Suzanna Low-Beer lists the following as essential characteristics of a jūnzǐ:

> "The jūnzǐ…takes in a given situation, extracts essential information, and acts on that information with confidence…
>
> …is of value to the community while maintaining personal power,
>
> …provides a proven means to cultivate self-trust (devotion) and focus (knowledge) to the highest level possible."[31]

The first of these characteristics is somewhat in line with the initial definition presented by Ritsema and Karcher, as person who conducts his or her life in accordance with the Dao as revealed through clear and proper divination. It will be discussed in greater detail in another section of this text.

The third characteristic is primarily concerned with the proper cultivation of human qualities (in the form of self-trust, devotion, and so on) as well as a general cultivation of qì within oneself. These will be discussed below.

This leaves us with the second clause: "[being] of value to society while [at the same time maintaining] one's own power." It seems that the way to gloss this idea of "power" is most properly done by the use of the term "dé" (德) (virtue, power, attribute, etc.). This is one of

---

30 Rudolf Ritsema and Stephen Karcher, *I Ching: The Classical Oracle of Change—the First Complete Translation with Concordance* (New York: Barnes & Noble, 1995).

31 Susanna Low-Beer, "The Superior Physician: Medical Practice as Seen Through the *Yijing's* Junzi, Part I," (2009): https://classicalchinesemedicine.org/wp-content/uploads/2010/03/lowbeer_yijing_I.pdf [Last accessed 26 Nov 2020].

the major points of consideration for enacting and embodying benevolent behavior. Give to others, but do not deplete your own stores. Done in the proper way, benevolence can only foster the giver and the receiver.

She further goes on to say: "The jūnzǐ (君子) of the Yijing is a person who recognizes himself as an instrument of heaven [i.e., the Dao] whose main purpose is to help others."[32] To do so at the expense of one's own potential or power depletes one, and lessens his or her ability to give to others (i.e., to act with regard to others). The Daoist is unconcerned with the "moral" aspects of benevolence which find purchase in Confucian thought and is much more concerned with the doing of the things which allow others to be "free and easy."

So what is one to do?

Give some of your time to those who would benefit from it. Volunteer time freely to persons in need of resources or mentoring. Serve the homeless by cooking food. Teach someone how to read, or any skill that will add depth and the chance for participation to a life. You can certainly give resources to a cause and still embody benevolence. At this stage, though, be with the people who you are called to help. Be among others so that you can observe what is being done.

Next observe within yourself what is the net effect, and what is the most prominent affect at play.

Do you find contentedness in the embodiment that you have currently chosen in relation to others?

Are you frustrated? If so, why?

Are you bored or impatient with the process of being around others?

What does the body feel like during your examination of these feelings?

Do you feel extremely tired, or generally depleted afterward? Jagged? Energized? If you feel tired, jagged, or uptight, this is a reliable sign that the qì has become stagnated within the system of the body and mind, or that it is being given or taken to freely. There are times when one must learn to pull away and to renew oneself in order that they are able to continue serving others.

32 *Ibid.*

To Be Humane

Benevolence as it is laid out in the model of the "learned gentleman" or jūnzǐ is best practiced invisibly. It is not that one's actions are not seen, but that one is doing what is natural, without elaborate performance. The humaneness which comes from this comes in showing others by sincere and unflattering example. In this way, not only does the individual who gives effort to another becom more a part of the world around them, but other people around them become likewise transformed, so that they too, want to grace others with a quiet benevolence which asks little in return.

稚子气概：

找到自己就是坐在一個與明，命運和命運相稱的空間中。

每個人都必須選擇自己的方式到達那裡…

Zhìzǐ Qìgài:

Zhǎodào zìjǐ jiùshì zuò zài yīgè yǔ míng, mìngyùn hé mìngyùn xiāngchèn de kōngjiān zhōng.

Měi gèrén dōu bìxū xuǎnzé zìjǐ de fāngshì dàodá nàlǐ...

脆骨：

我們不會選擇我們的出生地，出生對象和條件。

這是我們每個人都必須開始的地方。

Cuìgú:

Wǒmen bù huì xuǎnzé wǒmen de chūshēng dì, chūshēng duìxiàng hé tiáojiàn.

Zhè shì wǒmen měi gèrén dōu bìxū kāishǐ dì dìfāng.

稚子气概：

該人必須盡最大可能選擇一個人會在何時何地參與到誰手中，參與時間長短。

選擇父母或祖先的道路並不構成犯罪，但人道的人必須選擇它。 否則，就會陷入困境。

Zhìzǐ Qìgài:

Gāi rén bìxū jǐn zuìdà kěnéng xuǎnzé yīgèrén huì zài héshí hé de cānyù dào shuí shǒuzhōng, cānyù shíjiān chángduǎn.

Xuǎnzé fùmǔ huò zǔxiān de dàolù bìng bù gòuchéng fànzuì, dàn réndào de rén bìxū xuǎnzé tā. Fǒuzé, jiù huì xiànrù kùnjìng.

脆骨：

選擇合適的空間會使耕作更加困難，或者使耕作成為可能。如果真的做到的話，選擇環境本身就是耕種。

Cuìgú:

Xuǎnzé héshì de kōngjiān huì shǐ gēngzuò gèngjiā kùnnán, huòzhě shǐ gēngzuò chéngwéi kěnéng. Rúguǒ zhēn de zuò dào dehuà, xuǎnzé huánjìng běnshēn jiùshì gēngzhòng.

On Choosing Your Environment

"Baby's Breath":

To find oneself is to sit in a space that accords with one's Ming, both the light and the fate.

Each must choose his or her own way to get there, truly, but each must ultimately choose to be (t)here.

It is in doing this that we find our communities, or our chosen quiet solitude.

Each requires a recognition of place, and from whence experience can spring fresh and free.

"Brittle Bones":

It is daring to say this, Little One.

To propose that we should each choose where we are is a difficult plow to pull.

We do not choose where we are born, to whom, and under what circumstance.

This is the point from which each of us must begin.

Not all beginnings are equal! It cannot be ignored.

"Baby's Breath":

It is no failure of a person to endure his or her circumstance early in life, nor is it necessarily a shortcoming or a boon to endure circumstance later in life.

The person must choose, as best as one is able where, when, and with whom one will become involved, and for how long.

To choose the path taken by one's parents or ancestors is no crime, but the humane person must choose it. To do otherwise is to become stuck.

This is one sign of a ghost.

"Brittle Bones":

To find a ghost or to find a saint is often just the matter of a few steps forward or backward, left or right. The act of cultivation is repetition in either case.

Choosing the right space can make cultivation more difficult, or it can enable it. If done truly, choosing your environment can be cultivation in itself.

If you would become a ghost, go where they are, if you wish to become a sage, go where they are.

This is choosing one's environment.

COMMENTARY

THERE IS MUCH that we can accomplish on our own. Our own effort can carry us far, particularly when any kind of deep self-cultivation is at hand. There are, however, many other factors which can affect the outcome of personal endeavors, environment being only one.

In being around people, we can often be influenced by their action or inaction.

In their own ways, spaces are also alive, with their own agency or inertia.

In being in certain environments, our experience can likewise be stifled or invigorated. Repetition, response, and repetition once more of engrained patterns can take place just outside of awareness, as we go on "autopilot" within some set of circumstances.

> Familiarity is a source of comfort, after all. When we can only envision ourselves within our chosen space to the point of excluding other possibilities, it has become a point of focus for our ghostly side, and will sustain it. The prospect of quitting our haunts can produce anxiety deep within us, as we are left vulnerable. Often, like-minded ghosts can be found in these environments, and if we can tolerate company, it will serve to reinforce those habits, thoughts, or situations which contributed to the initial steps along the path of the ghost.[33]

It is vitally important, then, that we learn to recognize our "haunts" and to acknowledge their effect on our experience. Further, if we are in the position to do so, we should strive to find and foster those places that contribute to an enriched awareness of the world around each of us. Good or bad spaces to not exist as such. It is the habituation and habit of the beings within it that are of greatest import.

33 John Anderson, *The Way of the Living Ghost* (Seattle: Revelore Press, 2019), 289.

The Embodiment

There are several stages of participation in the lesson behind this passage. Each of these points of interaction with a space can and will affect how the inhabitants of the space will react to it. These can include:

- Recognition of Space
- Recognition of Interaction/Choice (Like attracts like, what are the inhabitants "bringing" to the space itself)
- Clearance/Remediation (If necessary)
- Inception and sustenance of Flourishing/ Vibrant/"Easy"/Nourishing Spaces

Recognition of Space

When one enters into a space, there is, at some level, the acknowledgement of the atmosphere and composition of a place. The composition of place here is meant to convey the physicality of a place within space. That is, its orientation (position in relation to other things): Where is it? What is it made of? When was it "opened" as a space? What is or was its purpose, how is the space used currently, and how was it used in the past? What is/are the current population(s) of the space?

The atmosphere of a place can be much more difficult to pinpoint. It can encompass things such as reputation (infamous or otherwise), as well as the subtler effects that a place can have on inhabitants (gut feelings, "hidden" smells/sounds, established presence of the space ("The house didn't like me." "It wanted me out." etc.; the space seems to be "alive in itself."), etheric textures or even "layers" of inhabitants over time. Here, there is only the recognition that a place has an existence of its own, with its own boundaries and life cycle.

Much of this type of interaction with space may occur without really becoming part of the space. The next point of contact with place begins the process of drawing in inhabitants and interacting with them.

JOHN ANDERSON

Recognition of Interaction/Choice

For most of us, there is a point at which we begin to identify with a space. It becomes "ours" and we begin to establish some level of ownership of or attachment to the space. It is at this point that our fates become intertwined with the features and fortunes of a place, for better or worse.

By our nature, most of us will seek out places which are similar in quality and temperament to ourselves, or are at least familiar to us. It's fair to say that we all have entered a place and felt a sense of belonging or even kinship with the space. Under most circumstances we learn to enjoy it, the ambiance, the comings-and-goings of others associated with the place.

If a space is not well kempt or if the inhabitants engage in behaviors characterized within the idea of grasping as it is found in Buddhism, the space will eventually begin reach out to search for other inhabitants to fill it.

Any place that sees humans at the extremes of their emotions or health is easily affected in this manner.

Clearance/Remediation (If Necessary)

There are spaces which go unused or misused for such an extended period that they begin to affect the areas which surround them. "Blight" is commonly used to describe this effect within urban settings. Any space is subject to this by way of contagion. If you wish to establish yourself within a space, you may find it necessary to clear away unwanted ambiance, atmosphere, or influence and to "remake" the space.

Clearance may be as mundane as cleaning a space to rid it of loose refuse, demolition to remove unwanted or unhealthy structures (think of the effect that mold or mildew might have, or the presence of pests which might compromise the integrity of the structure). It might also take subtler work to purify the space from undesired residual influence. In many cultures, this is most readily accomplished through the use of fumigation (i.e., "smudging") with various substances such as cedar or the ever-popular white sage as is used among many indigenous groups of North America, or Qinghao or Aiye (artemisia), or even frankincense and myrrh. The choice of substance varies widely depending on one's traditions, preferences, and capacities. Washes are also used for this purpose and can include varieties of rue and basil and other pungent substances. When availing yourself of this manner of work take sensitivities and allergies into account.

Inception and Sustenance of Flourishing/ Vibrant/"Easy"/Nourishing Spaces

In a more benign sense, the naming and ownership of a place can affect the inhabitants. Certainly, events such as assuming ownership of a first home can rewrite one's identity as a person, as can opening a new storefront. So, too, steps taken to reidentify a space can change the way in which it affects others. To this end, it may be desirable, or even necessary to rename a space in order to establish its connection with its new purpose as a "container" for the collective work or goals of the inhabitants who use the space.

Changing the physical appearance of a space can also delineate its new life. Paint and decoration may do wonders. So, too, opening up the space, even working to intentionally open the space.

In all of these cases, though, the work is done so that the inhabitants begin to reestablish and redefine their own relationships with the space, so that both the space and the inhabitant benefit from each other.

Intentional participation in a space may be a formalized performative act (as with a ribbon-cutting ceremony or the breaking of earth for the inception of a new structure) or it may be quite informal, as when a sports team might touch some part of the wall or door before beginning a game or match.

Acknowledge the spaces that you inhabit and the effect that they have on you. Notice your habits within commonly visited locales. Do you spend more money than you would in similar places? Be mindful of any moods visited upon you as you occupy a space, as you may be carrying them with you long after you leave, for better or worse. In this way, spaces may begin to affect other aspects of your life.

Greet the spaces you use as you would greet acquaintances or old friends. Some spaces will be met with proper etiquette while others are met with relaxed affection. Notice how you are received in return.

Homesickness

There is an aspect of place that has become a silent companion to many of us within modern societies. It is a reflection of oneself within a space, and a loss of that reflection of oneself. Homesickness is a yearning or nostalgia for a space, and usually at a particular time.

A certain sound.

A turn of phrase.

A smell.

A flavor.

All of these can elicit a visceral, deep, emotional response which one cannot fully control, but one can often learn to recognize and utilize the emotional force of this encounter in the space and time.

Gather material from the space which elicits this response as you become aware of it.

A brick.

Gather a large handful of soil, grass, flowers, and the like from the space.

Gather these materials from new places that you begin to inhabit.

Revisit these if and when one feels a tug at the Heart.

This is one approach, of course. Seeing any space as alive allows one to gain relation to it, and in this way, it allows belonging, as well.

In the Daoist worldview, "home" is coming to the place where one presently exists, at the intersections between Yin and Yang, and even within the open void from which all things can come forth. In this text, "home" is the Xīn as the center of awareness and coherence. It is both illusionary and essential. The paradox is where the work is done.

To Be Humane

Each of us has this: Being born in place and often many of us not feeling as if we belong anywhere. To be humane is to recognize this as a possibility for everyone, and acknowledging this in equanimity for ourselves and others.

The goal here though is to belong everywhere, and it is possible through the work of the Shén, centered in the space of the Xīn.

稚子气概：

我們注定要平衡陰和陽這兩個原則。

這是我們在這個地方的約會。

這就是為什麼人類必須自覺地參與這兩個原則。

每個包含另一個的種子。

Zhìzǐ Qìgài:

Wǒmen zhùdìng yào pínghéng yīn hé yáng zhè liǎng gè yuánzé.

Zhè shì wǒmen zài zhège dìfāng de yuēhuì.

Zhè jiùshì wèishéme rénlèi bìxū zìjué de cānyù zhè liǎng gè yuánzé.

Měi gè bāohán lìng yīgè de zhǒngzǐ.

脆骨：

切勿使陰陽狀態遠離您的心靈。

陰和陽是萬種萬物的基礎和根基，但是如果要同時維持經驗和存在，那麼這三件事是永遠不可能的⋯

Cuìgú:

Qiè wù shǐ yīnyáng zhuàngtài yuǎnlí nín de xīnlíng.

Yīn hé yáng shì wàn zhǒng wànwù de jīchǔ hé gēnjī, dànshì rúguǒ yào tóngshí wéichí jīngyàn hé cúnzài, nàme zhè sān jiàn shì shì yǒngyuǎn bù kěnéng de...

On Yin and Yang

"Baby's Breath":

The *Daodejing* tells us that we ought to be receptive and passive if we are ever to reach an understanding of the Dao.

If we do this, it says we will be as the Earth.

The Earth is the utmost Yin.

We cannot do only this.

Even to be in accord with Heaven is to know utmost Yang.

This, too, is beyond human nature.

We are meant to balance the two principles of Yin and Yang.

This is our appointment in this place.

This is why humans must participate consciously in both principles; each contains the seed of the other.

Let one reach the zenith and begin its fall, while the other reaches the apogee and begins its flight.

Both Yin and Yang must rise and fall.

The opposition of natural disposition allows for continued mutability.

"Brittle Bones":

Never keep the state of Yin and Yang far from your Mind.

Yin and Yang are the base and the root of all the ten thousand things, but there are three things which they can never be if both experience and existence are to be sustained:

Neither Yin nor Yang can be alone,

Neither Yin nor Yang can be pure,

Neither Yin nor Yang can remain still.

The result of any of these is either illusion or death.

Pay attention to the silken thread where Yin and Yang intermingle!

Here, there is great tumult and thunder and the thrum of lives lived.

The result of this union is the coming and going of the Ten-Thousand Things.

COMMENTARY

THE WAY BEGOT ONE,
AND THE ONE, TWO;
THEN THE TWO BEGOT THREE
AND THREE, ALL ELSE.
—DAODEJING, CHAPTER 42

THE INTERPLAY BETWEEN the contractile, passive force of Yin and expansive, active force of Yang has remained one of the underpinning ontological propositions for many forms of Eastern philosophy for many thousands of years, with paired lists of attributes and qualities dating back to at least the third century BCE.[34] Perhaps no philosophical framework has come to rely on these two "universal" principles as means to understand the world and one's place within it more than Daoism.

While it is true that most in the West are familiar with the terms Yin and Yang, it would be fair to say that most of us have neither the comprehension, nor the appreciation for these two principles beyond Yang as "male" and "active" and Yin as "female" and "passive." While these are not incorrect in the simplest reading of the terms, there is much more to unpack theoretically, and much that might be of practical use. Let us begin by examining Yin and Yang as broader concepts.

Yang	Yin
Heaven	Earth
Sun	Moon
Light	Darkness
Fire	Water
Energy	Matter
Activity	Rest

34 Fabrizio Pregadio, "Yin and Yang," Golden Elixir, 2019: https://www.goldenelixir.com/taoism/yin_and_yang.html [Accessed on December 1, 2020].

Generates	Grows
Expansion	Contraction
Rising	Descending
Above	Below
Male	Female

Regarding this ever-present pair, four main points of theory are vital to understanding their interplay:

- Opposition
- Interdependence
- Consumption
- Inter-transformation

Yin and Yang as Relative Opposites

They are either on the opposite ends of a cycle, like the seasons of the year, or, opposites on a continuum of energy or matter. This opposition is relative and can only be spoken of in relationships. For example: Water is Yin relative to steam but Yang relative to ice. Yin and Yang are never static but in a constantly changing balance.

Interdependence of Yin and Yang

The Tai Ji (Supreme Ultimate) diagram shows the relationship of Yin & Yang and illustrates interdependence on Yin & Yang. Nothing is totally Yin or totally Yang. Just as a state of total Yin is reached, Yang begins to grow. Yin contains seed of Yang and vise versa. They constantly transform into each other. For example: no energy without matter, no day without night. The classics state: "Yin creates Yang and Yang activates Yin."

Mutual Consumption of Yin and Yang

Relative levels of Yin Yang are continuously changing. Normally this is a harmonious change, but when Yin or Yang are out of balance they affect each other, and too much of one can eventually weaken (consume) the other.

There are four (4) possible states of imbalance:

- Preponderance (Excess) of Yin
- Preponderance (Excess) of Yang
- Weakness (Deficiency) of Yin
- Weakness (Deficiency) of Yang

Fire and water provide the most common illustration of this pairing with relation to the four states of imbalance.

In the first instance, if the soil is very wet and the weather is rainy (excess Yin), it would be more difficult to start a fire even with proper fuel.

In the second instance, it is difficult to put out a raging fire (excess Yang). Even if weather patterns are within normal ranges, large forest fires require much effort to extinguish.

In the third instance, that of Yin deficiency, there is not enough water to put out even a small fire. This would be the equivalent of a drought.

In the fourth and final instance, this would be like trying to start a fire without any sort of ignition or friction. There is not even enough to start the process.

Inter-transformation of Yin and Yang

Both Yin and Yang can change into one another, but it is not a random event. Under healthy conditions, this mutual transformation from Yang to Yin and from the Yin to Yang will happen only when the time is right. Once Yang has ascended to its utmost it will begin naturally to fall. Once Yin has reached its greatest depths it will begin to ascend. The ability for this dynamic to take place rests with the fact that Yin provides the incipient kernel of Yang while Yin contains the smallest spark of Yang. This assures the continued transformation of the two principles into their opposites. Such is the connection of Yin and Yang.

For example: the fresh exuberance of Spring only occurs when the stillness and "death" of Winter has run its full course. When fresh growing plants die the physical material of those now gone plants will naturally return to the soil.

The awareness of Yin and Yang through the working of the Shén is the beginning point of so much other work, and while this text does not strive to work as an initiatory framework, the recognition of the co-mingling of Yin and Yang and action in accordance with this constant dynamism are revelatory in their own way.

The Embodiment

In the pairs listed above, we find what are largely considered polar dichotomies which are both relative and entirely theoretical. The upshot for an entity is much more complex by comparison.

Humans and other biological entities all have specific physiological correlates to Yin and Yang which can determine, to a great extent, the capacity that one has for physiological, psychological, and even spiritual endeavors as well as the development of the body itself.

> [T]he Yin and the Yang of the heart and the kidneys are transformations of the essence and the blood of one's father and mother at the time of their conjunction. They are provided with breath (qì) and substance; therefore they follow the body, and they either are there or are not there.[35]

The Manifestation of Yin and Yang in the Body

Each of the zàng organs has within it a manifestation of both Yin and Yang. These functional forms of Yin and Yang guarantee that the organ is dynamic, active, and sustained.

JOHN ANDERSON

35 Fabrizio Pregadio, "Yin and Yang," Golden Elixir, 2019: https://www.goldenelixir.com/taoism/yin_and_yang.html [Accessed on December 1, 2020].

The state of the Xīn and the Shén spirit is determined to a large part by the intimate, subtle balance between Heart Yin and Heart Yang.

Heart Yang provides the raw propulsive force needed to sustain and control the rhythmic movement of the heart as a component of functional qì within the vessels (mài, 脉), and thus, it also quickens and warms the blood within the vessels. This Yang allows the spirits energy and space to move both within and without physical boundaries of the body proper. In addition, it helps to keep boundaries. In this sense, it is able to assure that the cohesion and coherence of the spirits remains intact, and that they do not stray too far. In this sense, the Yang is protective, as it provides the energy necessary for containment.

Heart Yin provides the substance necessary for the flesh of the Xīn and the physical fluidity of the parenchyma to take form. The Yin is the physical last structure itself as well as the substances needed to sustain that physical structure. It is the centering gravity of being, and a locus for existence. It is also the means by which Yang is anchored and fed.

Earlier, we discussed Yang as a potential of qì or energy which ought to be conserved if we are to live healthy and colorful lives. We will touch on analogous themes for Yin later in the text.

What is essential in this passage is the theme of letting Yin and Yang connect, interact, consume, and transform.

The nature of Pure Yang is to rise, but if it remains pure will never be caught.

The nature of Pure Yin is to sink, but if it remains pure, it will never be moved.

Therefore, work to make the Yang descend and anchor it to its place.

Therefore, also work to make Yin ascend, but as if on a tether.

Attend to the working of Yin and Yang within you. There are a small handful of activities already touched upon which detail some work with the Yang principle, and the passages which detail nourishment, rest, and stillness provide insight into the Yin as an incarnated principle.

Ask yourself what is Yin and what is Yang in a given situation, and how are they intertwined with one another in the moment.

Everything can be broken down according to Yin and Yang, but only relative to conditions of more or less. The lived condition of Yin or Yang requires them to be together.

Contemplate this space of interaction.

Another means to understand the permutations of Yin and Yang is to study the *Yijing* or "Book of Changes." This classic text of Chinese divination uses a system of whole and broken lines as illustrations of Yin and Yang, with bifurcated lines representing the Yin principle and "complete" lines representing the Yang principle.

The "Invisible" Manifestations of Yin and Yang

Even immaterial and unseen forces and abstract concepts are beholden to the interplay between Yin and Yang. Justice must balance between the relatively Yang expression of punishment versus the Yin component of restitution. Love can possess a Yang quality, wherein two lovers pine for one another and meet explosively, or it can take on a Yin quality wherein a mother has compassion and nurturing as manifestation of love for her child.

Even the spirits have Yin and Yang components which are complementary to one another in the forms of jīngshén (精神) and shénqí (神奇).

Jīngshén is that aspect of a spirit which allows it to act on and within the world. It is the conjoining of the material essence (jīng; 精) with the ephemeral nature of the Shén spirits which provides them a "body" or "form." The shénqí is the empowering mandate from Heaven, the spark of the ineffable and the numinous used by the spirits to act upon the world.

To Be Humane

There is no human virtue to Yin and Yang.

There is no inherently human experience to the play between Yin and Yang. The two exist as potential *and* they exist as functional substances within the body. Just as blood and qì are vital constituents of form, so too Yin and Yang find expressions in the body. Most appropriate to the discussion of Shén are the Heart Yin and Heart Yang which served to provide the viscous medium which lubricates the parenchyma of the Heart and it provides the raw energetic impulse necessary to keep the Heart beating.

If anything, any sort of discussion of Yin and Yang in the human sphere should center around preservation of the two and maintaining the counterbalance, connection, interdependence, and mutual transformation, as these all relate to a lived human life, for it is in the play of these two principles that life emerges.

稚子气概

陰必須漂浮才能傳播，

楊必須下降才能被保持。

Zhìzǐ Qìgài:

Yīn bìxū piāofú cáinéng chuánbò, yáng bìxū xiàjiàng cáinéng bèi bǎochí.

脆骨：

必須使陽沉入，陰必須輕柔地上升。

這就是為什麼火必須從底部開始，而云則是從天空而不是土壤中積聚雨水。

Cuìgú

Bìxū shǐ yáng chén rù, yīn bìxū qīngróu dì shàngshēng.

Zhè jiùshì wèishéme huǒ bìxū cóng dǐbù kāishǐ, ér yún zé shì cóng tiānkōng ér bùshì tǔrǎng zhōng jījù yǔshuǐ.

On Bringing Forth

"Baby's Breath":

We have talked of Yin and Yang.

By their natures, one floats and one sinks.

This is not proper!

Yin must float in order to disseminate,

And Yang must descend in order to be kept.

"Brittle Bones":

In the Book of Permutations, Heaven and Earth interact naturally, but this does not imply ease.

Up is up, and down is down.

Here, the Fire and Water, become the living powers of Heaven and Earth. They must naturally be reversed.

Yang must be caused to submerge, and Yin must softly ascend.

This is why Fire must start from a base, and clouds amass rainwater from the sky rather than from the soil.

Still, fiery comets from the sky and fast-moving floods seeping into the soil do not always bring the gladdest tidings.

"Baby's Breath":

So it is within each of us.

The movement of Qián (乾) and Kūn (坤), of the ineffable Taiji can only issue forth within each of us as the essential movement of Fire and Water, properly cultivated, cared for, and contained.

"Brittle Bones":

Suspend your potencies,

Upend Yin and Yang,

Hang them, but upside down,

If you want to bring them into the world.

COMMENTARY

The Emptiness from which existence comes forth is the central hub; Qián (乾) and Kūn (坤) are the axle passing through the hub, which holds the wheel in position; and the wheel with its spokes represents the compass of space and the cycles of time governed by Water and Fire. The wheel, therefore, is the frame (ti: 體) that enables Emptiness to operate (or "function"; yong: 用) throughout space and time.[36]

The Fire (Yang) and Water (Yin) are brought to bear within the world as an initial awareness dictated by clear and open function of the singular Shén spirit, hosted in the Heart , which collects and organizes our perceived reality into a coherent, (if not always orderly) whole.

We are a part of this whole, too, and our Shén spirits are deeply entangled with this dynamic of Emptiness and function, of Yin and Yang, of Water and Fire, and of Earth and Heaven—but only so far as we let these come forth into the lived world that is the present moment.[37]

This is the duty of the Shén spirit of the Heart.

To Be Seen

There is a Chinese term (rén; 仁) that denotes a basic human quality, a "humanness" with which we are imbued (or perhaps conferred) at some point during gestation. We are of course imbued with a number of attributes which qualify us as "human": a physical form, "inner" nature, the "seven emotions" (qīqíng; 七情), cognitive capacities which allow us to evaluate and calculate, and lastly, a Shén or "spirit"

---

36 Fabrizio Pregadio, "Creation and Its Inversion: Cosmos, Human Being, and Elixir in the 'Cāntóng qì [參同契]' (The Seal of the Unity of the Three)," in Anna Andreeva and Dominic Steavu, (eds.), *Transforming the Void: Embryological Discourse and Reproductive Imagery in East Asian Religions* (Leiden: Brill, 2015), 186–211.

37 The Hún spirit (魂), the ethereal representative of the Wood Phase within us has a presence with the Shén spirit. The Hún resides in a space of future possibilities, vision, and planning and is bound to the "nowness" of the Shén. It is extant in a now of concretized futures, and it exists in the futures not yet set. The two can be visualized as a Venn diagram consisting of "present" and "future," with the intersecting space equivalent to the immanent future.

which broadly speaking is often held within the Chinese culture as an imprint of divine mandate and the open-ended duties with which we are all subsequently charged as this mysterious mandate unfolds. Many of these qualities are easily recognized and acknowledged within Confucianism, Daoism, and Buddhism, widely recognized as the three main currents of premodern religious expression within China.

There is, though, another concept at play when one speaks of humanness (rén; 仁). It is a concept that is perhaps a bit more difficult to grasp, partly because of the linguistic qualities of the Chinese language, and partly because it is not a concept that was widely recognized until a close relative, a small turn of phrase, made its wider appearance in English.

"I feel seen."

In the easiest terms this means: "I recognize that someone has acknowledged an important aspect of myself."

Thus, humanity requires something else, it requires the quality of being able to be seen in the first place. This concept, known as jian (见 or 見), is often used to refer to something as being recognizable, observable, able to be apprehended or comprehended. In modern use, jian is most often applied to inanimate objects.

Common definitions for jiàn include:

- To see or to look at
- To meet
- To appear to be a thing

As well as:

- To perceive
- To comprehend
- To experience
- *To be seen or glimpsed*
- *To be visible, to show forth*

The last two of these definitions are of particular interest for this passage, as they imply the natural capacity for being seen, of being visible to others, and of showing forth. According to Daoist teacher Ming Liu.[38] It is this last gloss for jian, that of showing forth, which has the greatest implication for the discussion of the virtue of humanity (rén: 仁) contained herein, as it alse requires that one also possesses the quality of míng (明) or "brightness" which comes from within.

As a quality in humans, this trait of jian allows us to be recognized by others. When friends see us in our physicality, we are said to possess jian, and when we are "recognized" according to the value of our inner lives, we have jian. Jian is a measure of the weight of one's existence. It is the fundamental recognition by others of one's being.

Thus, jian is a quality which articulates the gravity of our being expressed as a presence within the world for others to experience. It is also therefore part of our presence with ourselves and the interiority of our existence. It is not, however, something that need only apply to another person. This can also be turned inwardly.

If I am unable to acknowledge parts of my own experience, this indicates that my own jian is diminished—I am unable to see certain parts of myself.

Thus, in order for me to recognize the presence of others, I must also be able to recognize and participate in my own presence, my own gravitas, influence, and agency within the world. Only then can that being-in-itself exude out (and in) as is the charge of the Xīn and the "Cinnabar Spirit" which resides therein.

The Shén both receives and issues forth.[39]

This is the true pivot of the spirits.

---

38 Born Charles Belyea (1947–2015).

39 To visualize this, imagine a torus (a doughnut-shaped figure that is revolving and which has no measurable hole in the center. It would rotate outward on the top and inward on the bottom, even though it is one continuous surface. The Xīn takes in and emits reality as the Shén moderates it.

Embodiment

Once again, we come into contact with one of the most quintessential paradoxes of human existence. What is it to be conscious? What is it to have awareness? It is the ability to take in sensorium and to let it issue forth from us in return. There is no bringing in without the outward thrust of awareness.

The purpose of embodiment in this passage is merely to recognize in detail the ways in which you see the world and the filters through which this can happen.

No one technique or exercise can illustrate this "going forth" specifically. The emergence and going forth is the outward movement of the Shén spirits is driven by the Yang principle. The return of the Shén spirits to the sanctum and succor of the physical body rests with the centripetal, localized denseness that is the Yin principle.

Do you know how it feels to be unseen in a situation? How do you experience the world in these situations?

What happens to the Shén spirit when you have been passed over or ignored *and wanted to be seen*?

How does this differ from a situation in which you were successful at "being seen" or not "being seen" when you wished to be invisible?

The first case—wanting to be but not being seen—might arise when Yang is not strong or bright enough to stand out *or* when there is too much Yin covering the senses of the observer.

The second case—that of not wanting to be seen—requires that one "dim the lights," suppressing Yang so as to fall into the background

How does the world issue forth when the environment is different? How do *you* issue forth when the environment is different?

All of this is a matter of carrying yourself into the world, knowing that the sheer act of existence carries a gravity of meaning. This showing forth, having the "weight" of being which causes others to "see" us, is an important duty of all of the spirits, and is one of the reasons they should be engaged with and cultivated.

To Be Humane

While we are being asked to acknowledge that awareness issues forth from us to some extent, this is also a call to recognize the limits of that awareness. To be human and to be humane require a recognition of capacities issuing forth from us, and a recognition of the limits of those same capacities. There is also the recognition that the vast majority of human beings share similar experiences, which are rooted in the issuing forth of awareness

脆骨：

不要害怕天使或魔鬼拴在你的背上。

並非這些事情會使您的精神不安並虹吸您的名聲。

實際上，這將是世俗的事情。

Cuìgú:

Bùyào hàipà tiānshǐ huò móguǐ shuān zài nǐ de bèi shàng.

Bìngfēi zhèxiē shìqíng huì shǐ nín de jīngshén bù'ān bìng hóngxī nín de míngshēng.

Shíjì shang, zhè jiāng shì shìsú de shìqíng.

稚子气概

最隱蔽的存在存在始於意識的喪失。

Zhìzǐ Qìgài:

Zuì yǐnbì de cúnzài cúnzài shǐ yú yìshí de sàngshī.

On Possession

"Brittle Bones":

Do not be afraid of the angels or the devils tethered to your back. It is not these things which will unsettle your spirit and siphon away your Ming.

In truth it will be the mundane things which do this.

It will be the everyday things, the small things repeated without awareness which will take up your time and experience the most.

You will only notice the larger things though. The things into which you've put your effort, sweat, and Blood.

And your pride.

"Baby's Breath":

This in itself is no evil thing.

It is good to do what you have to set out to do.

It is a more a matter of how well your performance proceeds. How naturally and easily does your work unfold? Not insofar as you are recognized by others, but how natural and easy your performance is. This is the essence of wu-wei, of doing without effort.

This is true no matter what the discipline.

The most insidious possession of being begins with a loss of awareness.

It is a loss of the awareness of self, which, while sometimes good, does not allow engagement with ourselves as a coherent whole, and further, does not fully allow engagement with the larger reality which surrounds each of us.

This first minuscule lapse of awareness allows pinholes to form in one's being, and for exterior agents to gain a foothold and thus affect the body and the mind.

COMMENTARY

IF ONE IS not vigilant and firm, pain and want both provide the keys to the inner gates of consciousness. These are the initial pangs which give rise to the Hunger that is felt so viscerally by many living ghosts, and it is from this point that control of the Heart-Mind (Xīn) can be usurped. In truth though, we do not need to have the Shén completely clouded over to experience something akin to possession.

The roots of possession of the mind and body begin with wants, needs, and distraction. The mind can be possessed, waylaid, and seized by any idea, person, or thing.

A promotion.

A lost love.

An involved project.

Acquiring a new house or a new car.

Any and all of these can preoccupy one to the extent that other areas of life suffer. For the Shén in its role as mediator and moderator of consciousness, this is possession in the simplest terms.

Possession then is not necessarily the inhabitation or infestation of the body by some ghost or devil. We can become possessed by anything. Possession occurs when an idea, a person, an item, a feeling begins to co-opt one's awareness and function.

If it is, however, the result of some external agency, there is likely to be resistance, if not overt opposition. It stems from some internal agency in disharmony. There is likely to be dissonance at the very least, as the spirits are left in disarray as they struggle to protect the coherence of the person from external agents.

The Embodiment

Pay attention to what is occurring around you in this immediate moment.

Be mindful of the sensations felt within the body and of the thoughts and emotions you are currently experiencing.

When awareness is focused within, the "inner" (yíng; 营) and "outer" (wéi; 围) qì harmonizes.[40]

Do you have difficulty in maintaining awareness of the present moment?

If so, are particular "themes" coming out? That is, is there a thing upon which you are fixated?

Write down or otherwise solidify those things which are usurping your consciousness. Name them if necessary.

Speak to them.

How do the Hún, the Shén, and the Pò react in this moment of realization?

When you do find yourself drifting toward the object which possesses you, or more likely, when you find yourself suddenly immersed in it, return to the breath and the heartbeat.

To Be Humane

It may be difficult to grasp how a discussion centering around possession, or rather around avoiding possession could provide insight as to how one might become more human in the Daoist use of the term.

The key lies in observing just where it is that our awareness is pulled on a day-to-day basis *and* in understanding how our boundaries can be affected by our awareness. When we are possessed, even in the most minor sense, we are not in full control of ourselves because we have lost awareness on some level. Given time and the right circumstances, this will result in a lessening, or perhaps, a loosening of capacity of the spirit of the Heart (the Shén) to maintain coherence of a fractal self.

How does one maintain awareness in the world as well as the social boundaries necessary to maintain coherence of one's own being while still resolving to grow, move, and change with spontaneity, ease, and newness?

40 The yíngqì provides the nourishment for the body, the mind, and the Shén spirits, while the wéi qì provides warmth and movement to the exterior muscles, skin, and hair, as well as providing the exterior "field" with which pathogens and exterior entities must contend if they are to establish contact with, attach to, or infest a body.

脆骨：

警惕人群剝奪自發性並控制經驗的力量。

在很多時候，最好找到自己的方式。

Cuìgú:

Jǐngtì rénqún bōduó zìfā xìng bìng kòngzhì jīngyàn de lìliàng.

Zài hěnduō shíhòu, zuì hǎo zhǎodào zìjǐ de fāngshì.

稚子气概：

我們在人群中感到安全，因為我們不再一個人呆著。

這不僅是因為我們需要其他人，他們的確認或批准印章。

沒有。

孤獨的恐懼之所以出現，是因為這個世界上的許多人不能在自己的公司中獨處。

Zhìzǐ Qìgài:

Wǒmen zài rénqún zhōng gǎndào ānquán, yīnwèi wǒmen bù zài yīgèrén dāizhe.

Zhè bùjǐn shì yīnwèi wǒmen xūyào qítā rén, tāmen dí quèrèn huò pīzhǔn yìnzhāng.

Méiyǒu.

Gūdú de kǒngjù zhī suǒyǐ chūxiàn, shì yīnwèi zhège shìjiè shàng de xǔduō rén bùnéng zài zìjǐ de gōngsī zhōng dúchǔ.

On Being with Others

"Brittle Bones":

Humans being can be a dangerous proposition, indeed!

They will steal your being-in-itself.

Be wary of the power of a crowd to take away your spontaneity and to control experience.

Much of the time it is better to find your own way.

Do not be fearful of this!

"Baby's Breath":

Most cannot find purchase on a lonely mountain.

The way of the hermit or anchorite is not for all.

This is not troublesome for the greater part of people. They will choose to be with others in order to feel related to others.

We feel safe in a crowd because we are no longer left on our own.

This is not just because we need others, their validation, or their seal of approval.

No.

This is not an expression either of clarity or of spontaneity.

To loathe oneself is illness,

And to hide among others to avoid it is common.

COMMENTARY

HUMAN BEINGS ARE social creatures. We naturally append ourselves to larger goals, ideals, and groups. This is perfectly fine. If we are social creatures, it is only natural to be part of a group, and thus, part of a society. It is "normal" and generally, normative, to seek out inter-relationship with others. Herein lies the beginnings of the social contract, and with it, the psychological and even physical sequalæ that invariably accompany it.

The broad Confucian premise is that societal cohesion and harmony are of the utmost importance to the human endeavor and that the needs of individuals are subordinate to the needs of the group to which they belong.

The depth of this interrelatedness, however, is rarely ever apparent when we are among the throngs of humanity.

Its true import lies in the recognition of how we experience ourselves when we are alone. This is the key to this passage: to be with others fully, learn to be with yourself fully. If you do this, you are less likely to lose yourself in the fickle nature of the crowd.

Minding other people's business is to be a fake; to mind your own business is to be genuine. Before rectifying others, we must first rectify ourselves…It is only by reflecting on ourselves that we can be free of delusion, but when we reflect [only] on others, freedom from delusion is impossible.[41]

It is not the being-with-others that inherently takes one away from the Human path. Social behavior and the connection that it provides, if practiced from a state of awareness and agency, is crucial to our well-being. If one constantly loses oneself in the masses, though, this is delusion. In delusion, we have little connection to our own solitary being, and this, in turn, makes it more difficult to be among the tóngrén (同人), "the gathered-alike people," in an authentic manner.

---

41 Yousheng Liu, *Let the Radiant Yang Shine Forth: Lectures on Virtue*, translated by Sabine Wilms and Liu Zuozhi, (Corbett: Happy Goat, 2014), 97.

In delusion, the voice and volition of the many becomes the voice and volition of the individual.

The Embodiment

There are two essential questions hinted at in this passage which each of us would do well to try to answer for ourselves:

First: "How do I feel when I am alone?"

Ask yourself.

How does the mind react to this question?

Is there an internal tension that arises when this question is asked? Is there dread? Isolation? A feeling of being overwrought?

On the other hand, is there a sense of contentment which accompanies the thought of time spent alone?

Make a record of these impressions in some manner, be it in a written form, a verbal form, or some other engagement of your senses.

For many, there is an unease, which for better or worse is at least tolerable. It is when this becomes a dis-ease with our selves that doubt and disaffection begin to prick at us; eventually it sets upon us like an unnerving itch inside that we can neither scratch nor disregard.

The initial recognition of this state (if it is indeed present) is the first step to transforming it.

And second: "How do I feel when I am in a group with which I share commonality?"

Do you feel at ease within your groups?

Do you have a "say," that is, a way in which you can affect the group to which you belong?

Do you feel as if you an outlier in some fashion?

How, and how does your body react to this?

Record these impressions.

The record of one's impressions is self-reflective, but it is not the goal, here. It is used as a means of priming you to examine your immediate experience so that you might better learn to recall the impressions felt or experienced in a particular situation so as to recognize similar states in the moment.

Let yourself be part of a crowd at a concert if that is what you choose. Participate in a political body if you believe in the message espoused. Experience belonging.

Lose yourself in the group *and* recognize its effect on you.

Also, learn to be alone with yourself.

Recognize the paradox of your self being in a state of emptiness among the fullness of the throngs.

To Be Humane

Find your groups, find your "tribe." Allow for belonging, but even here, do not compromise your nature or sacrifice your destiny to achieve it. When you are with others, help transform them even as you are changed by them, but be mindful of your "selves."

稚子气概

必須注意自我，特別是在與他人互動方面。

Zhìzǐ Qìgài:

Bìxū zhùyì zìwǒ, tèbié shì zài yǔ tārén hùdòng fāngmiàn.

脆骨：

可以參加團體的管理。

這可以。 但是要小心！

Cuìgú:

Kěyǐ cānjiā tuántǐ de guǎnlǐ.

Zhè kěyǐ. Dànshì yào xiǎoxīn!

On Governing the Self

"Baby's Breath":

Care must be taken with regards to the self, especially in relation to interactions with others.

Not just that a group of individuals can bend your ideas to suit its needs, but that more anomalous groups, more invisible groups can also have an impact on how you view the world and how you act within it.

"Brittle Bones":

It is permissible to participate in the governance of a group.

This is fine. But be wary!

Be mindful of the liege engines!

They, too, are weapons of war.

The same force that elevates kings,

Will also bury corpses.

Truly, they will take your freedom and your spontaneity in the name of a group for which they may care very little.

Only help govern others if you can govern yourself!

"Baby's Breath":

So it comes to this:

Each must choose his or her level of participation with any larger group. To be part of a society is to give part of oneself to the good of the group.

In many places, this is required, and the person is consumed by the larger drives of the assembled masses.

"Brittle Bones":

This is the way in much of the world.

The ancients point to the traits of the jūnzǐ, or educated person, as a means to strike a balance between the indi,vidual and the group, but as she leads by example, she only fully seeks to rein in her own conspiracy-of-one that is awareness.

COMMENTARY

THE WORK OF being in non-being allows one to harness the internal power which comes from self-governance. It is an internal power of one's being which not only informs the unfolding of one's life but also the quality of the lives around the person who is in accordance with her own power and the Dao. Furthermore, this internal power is a self-contained principle which has its own internal logic and organizational impetus. Low-Beer writes:

> This "power within something by which it expresses its true nature" is not simply a fixed quality, it is a dynamic entity, intrinsic to that which it defines, which could even be characterized as a process. The process of dé[42] is a coming into being, which is also called arising. How does the jūnzǐ integrate dé into his life? Through the way that he rules himself and influences others.[43]

The person who is turned toward cultivation and self-governance (as most Daoists would be) "comes along for the ride" as it were and does not always have much direct impact on or say in the process. Governing oneself requires letting the Dao move and not worrying about the goal that the self wants.

The way of the group in the West is to strive for distinction from the group as individuals while still clinging to a group for security and identity. The Dao teaches us to become part of the crowd while still maintaining one's openness and pliability, and any "governance" of the group in accordance with the Dao would also be subject to the same. The *Huainanzi* states:

---

42 In this case gaining an increased capacity for virtues both as right-behavior and as demonstrable force of being.

43 S. Low-Beer, "The Superior Physician: Medical Practice as Seen Through the Yijing's Junzi, Part 2," (2009): www.classicalchinesemedicine.org [Last accessed 20 March 2019].

The affairs of the world cannot be deliberately controlled. You must draw them out by following their natural direction. The alterations of the myriad things cannot be fathomed. You must grasp their essential tendencies and guide them to their homes.[44]

This is a gift to others to show that openness and spontaneity allow one to keep one's power whether one is meditating alone on a mountainside or among the crowd at a loud concert. The jūnzǐ works to show others by example, and this can only come when one is able to govern the self.

This "self," as a singular and definitive unit of personhood is tricky in its own right particularly within the Daoist context. Within the corpus of work attributed to Zhuangzi, selfhood, it seems, is tremendously murky.

The most common story given in the Zhuangzi to invoke the ineffability of the self—the smoke and mirrors that is "me"—is the parable of the butterfly. In this story, Zhuangzi asks whether "he" is watching a butterfly on the wing, or the dream of a man originating from the butterfly as it sleeps. There is a dissolution of the subject and the object, and any sense of a "true" self is tenuous.

At best, "I" amounts to a cheap trick which we use to organize our experience. The political and ethical self are fleeting, illusory, and are only a pale "trace" of the intrinsic, "foundational" self.[45]

For Zhuangzi and Laozi, it is this foundational self which ought to be cultivated, connected with, and cherished, but it is not of itself, tied to any one part of human experience.

To uncover the foundational self—the traceless self—one must conjoin with Dao via the proxy of nothingness. Our Dao- self is thus neither illusionary, dualistic, or an exterior other; rather, it is a mode of thinking about being sustained by the openness

44 John S. Major, et al. (Trans.), *The Huainanzi* (New York: Columbia University Press, 2010).
45 David Chai, "Nothingness and Selfhood in the *Zhuangzi*," *Bloomsbury Handbook of Early Chinese Ethics and Philosophy*, ed. Alexus McLeod, (New York: Bloomsbury Academic, 2019).

of nothingness. This authentic self is hence a reflection of the nameless, formless flourishing of Dao.[46]

The self is a participation with the Dao, through repeated stillness and use, both. Stillness is requisite for emptiness and immersion. The Zhuangzi states:

> Chang Ji said, "In focusing on himself, he uses his knowledge to reach his heart-mind, and uses his heart-mind to reach the constant heart-mind. Why do other things hold him in such high regard?" Confucius said, "Men do not mirror themselves in moving water but in water that is still. Only the still can use stillness to still others."[47]

The rendering provided by David Hinton of the same passage might be interpreted as somewhat more personal by comparison:

> [The sage] uses understanding to reach mind. [The sage] uses mind to reach timeless mind. So why to things gather around him?

> People can't see themselves in rushing water, Confucius began. They see themselves in still water, for only stillness can still stillness.[48]

The Heart-mind here becomes the timeless mind, and one is only concerned with immersion in the stillness rather than mirroring it to others.

Even still, the deeper, immanent self is manifestation independent of time which is moderated by the Heart-mind.

The Heart-mind alluded to here is nothing other than the Xīn, the deeper movement of the singular Shén enshrined in the physical heart. Just as we rush around as in moving water, the edges of the Heart-mind

46 *Ibid.*
47 *Ibid.*
48 Hinton, *Chuang Tsu.*

blur. It is only when we are able to still this whirlwind state that this Dao-as-Self can emerge. We thus refine the Self. In doing this, we use the stillness of the Dao-self and the heart-mind to show others by our example, as "[o]nly the still can use stillness to still others."

This is a fundamental paradox, that we each might have both a foundational self based on hewing to nothingness as a practice, which is based in the chaotic space of potentiality provided by the movement of the Dao, yet which also comes forward as a shade into the arenas of ethics, politics, (and I would add pedagogy in its many forms, as well), as a social interlocuter, in order that the formless becomes intimately and ultimately bound to the world as an exteriorized component of the groups to which one belongs. We should not, however, confuse the two.

In Zhuangzi's estimation, it is this Dao-as-self which allows for the growth of virtue and power which others cannot easily observe and is an open secret in the world. The self-among-others is that which other people are able to see and experience second-hand through the natural movement and carriage of the individual.[49]

And even here, we need to beware of the idea of the enduring Self, for this is the pitfall of many Ghosts, and the space which demarcates the Human Way from the Way of the Living Ghost is perilously narrow.

The Embodiment

A freedom stems from the lack of control so often accompanying the acknowledgement that the self is both impermanent and composite. That is, it is not altogether "mine" and while there is some semblance of internal coherence regulated by the Shén spirit, there are many facets of the "I" which are not always under conscious control. What is of use here is to bring together the self as a flexible yet coherent structure, and this requires letting go of a single self. There is coherence in the chaos of Hundun, the state of circumscribed chaos, as it is the cosmic background and the ever-present matrix of now.

49 Chai, "Nothingness and Selfhood."

Fall into it and reform anew.

If we are to take awareness of change and adaptation as one of our underpinning criteria for being human, we must allow that the self can shift and morph in accordance with the experience of the moment. The Dao-as-Self is not something which could "belong" to any of us, but we can participate in it, can be immersed in it, and that, as with water, which can be seen as a "...self-constituting and indivisible whole." There are nonetheless innumerable eddies and currents of the Dao-as-experience which can give direction and even shdifferent "selves."

Examine your many selves.

The you that is a parent, a child to your parents, a lover, a friend, a business partner, a business owner, a teacher, a plumber. Observe them.

What do these varied "selves" contribute to the "interior" you of inner dialogue? What ties these together? You. The only catch: there is no one You.

Do you have a sense of an intrinsic self which cannot be tarnished or changed which makes you, you?

If so, how do you interact with this part of your experience? We each do this differently.

What role to the five Shén have here, as contributors to your sense of self?

Write down any thoughts or impression regarding this idea of multiple selves and dialogue with the one's you find in yourself. If you spend some time at it, you will be surprised by how many of you there are.

To Be Humane

Acknowledge that, whether we intend to or not, we affect others through our behavior and can therefore have some sway over others, particularly if they are in a state of compromised coherence.

Lead by example.

This is governing others by learning to govern the self.

脆骨：

估計道，我們不過是草狗，

在"人類"世界中，並非所有人都具有同等的地位。

這可以適用於世系的祝福，但是我們所有人都承擔著某些被詛咒的重量，這些事件甚至在我們進入世界之前就已承載。

Cuìgú:

Gūjì dào, wǒmen bùguò shì cǎo gǒu,

zài "rénlèi" shìjiè zhōng, bìngfēi suǒyǒu rén dōu jùyǒu tóngděng dì dìwèi.

Zhè kěyǐ shìyòng yú shìxì de zhùfú, dànshì wǒmen suǒyǒu rén dōu chéngdānzhe mǒu xiē bèi zǔzhòu de zhòngliàng, zhèxiē shìjiàn shènzhì zài wǒmen jìnrù shìjiè zhīqián jiù yǐ chéngzài.

稚子气概

你會怪那些來過的人嗎？

你學了什麼，好還是壞？

如果我們要自發和平穩，我們每個人都必須解開

106

線程並放鬆行為的紐帶。

我們每個人都必須解開構成我們內心的線程。

Zhìzǐ Qìgài:

Nǐ huì guài nàxiē láiguò de rén ma?

Nǐ xuéle shénme, hào huán shì huài?

Rúguǒ wǒmen yào zìfā hé píngwěn, wǒmen měi gèrén dōu bìxū jiě kāi xiànchéng bìng fàngsōng xíngwéi de niǔdài.

Wǒmen měi gèrén dōu bìxū jiě kāi gòuchéng wǒmen nèixīn de xiànchéng.

脆骨：

檢查您從父母和祖父母那裡收到的行為－您可能是唯一擁有以下行為的人…

如果是這樣的話，您可能是唯一可以在您的生產線中糾正它們的人。

Cuìgú:

Jiǎnchá nín cóng fùmǔ hé zǔfùmǔ nàlǐ shōu dào de xíngwéi-nín kěnéng shì wéiyī yǒngyǒu yǐxià xíngwéi de rén...

rúguǒ shì zhèyàng dehuà, nín kěnéng shì wéiyī kěyǐ zài nín de shēngchǎnxiàn zhōng jiūzhèng tāmen de rén.

On Inherited Burden

"Brittle Bones":

It is dangerous to say we are equal.

In the reckoning of the Dao, we are but straw dogs,

And in the "human" world not all have equivalence.

This can apply to the blessings of lineage, but all of us carry some amount of cursed weight that events carry even before we can see into the world.

It is the consequence of the works of our ancestors and of theirs before them.

This is "inherited burden."

"Baby's Breath":

Do you blame those who have come before?

What were you taught, for better or worse?

Each of us must untangle the threads and loosen the knots of behavior if we are to be spontaneous and smooth.

Each of us must disentangle the threads which make up our own Hearts.

If we learn a behavior from a parent, it is our work to address it, to discard it, or to refine it. It is also our work to refuse to change. To only blame others is a lost opportunity.

This is not to say that the blame is on the carrier of burden, but that the responsibility for transmutation and movement, for untying or cutting through knots rests there.

"Brittle Bones":

The *Yijing* tells us of the consequences if we do not bring ourselves to uprightness:

> At death...the evil luck will be transferred to children and grandchildren.[50]

Examine the behaviors that you have received from your parents and grandparents—you may be the only one who has...

And if this is so, you may be the only one who can rectify them in your line.

---

50 Paul Carus and D. T. Suzuki *The Canon of Reason and Virtue: (Lao-tze's Tao Teh King) Chinese and English* (1906; La Salle: Open Court, 1913), 65: http://www.sacred-texts.com/tao/crv/index.htm.

COMMENTARY

THE CONCEPT OF karma is a loaded one, and one which is fraught with technicalities. The version of karma which is received from the various Buddhist traditions is one of personal consequences. One's actions have effect only on his or her life, and cannot be transferred or transmitted under mundane conditions. It is therefore a personal tally of one's life. In many Daoist traditions, this is not so or, at the very least, is incomplete.

The notion of "inherited burden" (chéngfù; 承負) can be dated to the later Han dynasty (second century CE), and is one of the underpinning ideas of Daoist soteriology.[51] The two are related, but are different in their focus.

Karma is the recognition of the effect of individual behaviors on an individual life; it cannot be foisted upon another person.

> Crimes committed by a person become karmic effects for that individual and that karmic burden will be carried through many lifetimes of the same person. It is not something that can be passed to someone else. It is said that the "sins of the parents become that of the children," but according to Buddhism this could never be so. In orthodox Buddhism at least the transgressions of our ancestors are not passed down to us. In that way, karma does not function on the level of society and this is the fundamental difference between Buddhism and Daoism when it comes to transgression and sin.[52]

By contrast, we can see inherited burden as:

An expression referring to the accumulation of all sorts of

JOHN ANDERSON

51 At least in this tradition, that places an emphasis on salvation.
52 Kikuchi Noritaka, "The Accumulation of Crime and Punishment: The Ancient Daoist Notion of 'Inherited Burden' and its Relevancy Today," *Journal of International Philosophy* 1 (2012): 194–99.

problems on various levels—cosmic, collective, familial, and individual—caused by the misconduct of past generations, and which the present generation, whether itself responsible for additional misdeeds or not, must face up to.[53]

Inherited burden, then, represents the transmission of transgression from person-to-person. It is in, this sense, a societal phenomenon rather than a personal one.

This passage recognizes the wrongs done by one's ancestors, and this is the starting point. It is not so much an acknowledgement of personal "karma" as we understand it in the West. It is a stamp put upon one by one's progenitors, and it is this which you must address.

Here we have a recognition of two processes. First, that an individual must work to correct or compensate for the actions of our mother, father, and grandparents. This is echoed in the 18th hexagram of the *Yijing*, "Rotting" (Gǔ, 蠱), which indicates the presence of transgressive behavior which causes a rotting or befoulment. The commentary of the lines provides an image of transgression within a familial setting specifically:

1. The first SIX, divided, shows (a son) dealing with the troubles caused by his father. If he be an (able) son, the father will escape the blame of having erred. The position is perilous, but there will be good fortune in the end.

2. The second NINE, undivided, shows (a son) dealing with the troubles caused by his mother. He should not (carry) his firm correctness (to the utmost).

3. The third NINE, undivided, shows (a son) dealing with the troubles caused by his father. There may be some small occasion for repentance, but there will not be any great error.

4. The fourth SIX, divided, shows (a son) viewingindulgently the troubles caused by his father. If he go forward, he will find cause to regret it.

5. The fifth SIX, divided, shows (a son) dealing with the troubles

53 Andreeva and Steavu, *Transforming the Void*, 62

caused by his father. He obtains the praise of using (the fit instrument for his work).

6. The sixth NINE, undivided, shows us one who does not serve
    either king or feudal lord, but in a lofty spirit prefers (to attend
    to) his own affair.

This text also provides a clue as to the means of restitution, as well.

There is a recognition that an individual must "work through" the
inherited burden passed down through the generations through the
signature imparted from the ancestors as essence. Indeed, it is only
in the image of the last line that the individual has finally reached a
point wherein (s)he is unfettered by the familial karma suggested in
the previous five lines.

The second recognition, which from a Western viewpoint should
likely come first, is that one ought to act with the awareness that his
or her actions will have an effect on the circumstances of life which
can be passed down to subsequent generations, either as jīng-essence,
as learned behaviors, or both. The effect of one's actions are the person's individual karma, the inertia of choices made and unmade.
If one is not careful and judicious, their karma becomes inherited.
There is thus the distinct risk of perpetuating the cycle of inherited
burden, while also adding to its weight.

To the work of inherited burden, there needs be redress. It comes
in waves, and from earliest experiences.

> Children learn most quickly that which is the most apparently
> violent and "powerful." So it is passed on across and along gen-
> erations. This is a transmission of energy—an inherited bur-
> den. This transmission of burden can be very difficult to break
> once it has been ignominiously bestowed upon an individual.[54]

Here is the rub: if it is inherited, it is not your own of your own. Even
still, we are asked to rectify it, though not necessarily reconcile with it.

---

54 Anderson, *The Way of the Living Ghost*, 257.

The Embodiment

Work your ancestral altar in order to summon the Pò. This altar is at the submerged fire, oft shown as being in the area of the lower back. Remember, though that it is internal, and that, as an altar to the Shén, it must be accessed through the Shén spirit. It is not necessarily a physical space that is taken up by the kidneys and the lumbar region. Rather, it is the internal space which we must access by going into our past and asking our ancestors to come forward. They're not even necessarily our ancestors, not in the direct line. They may instead be the long echoes of distant ancestors who existed well before the original insult and who, given time, can help to resolve it. In any case, the largest goal is to activate one's ancestor altar through work. This cannot be dodged or redirected.

One can only do, confront, accept, and transform.

Part of this work, too, is the recognition and active rectification of ancestral insult. At times, this requires that we must be willing to go into those spaces within each of us which are terrifying to us or which have been sealed off altogether.

Sometimes this means doing work on the behalf of another human being (i.e., through the act of providing a therapeutic encounter, through the act of providing and/or encouraging artistic outlet, or even through the act of hearing the story of another as well as being present with them). This way we can begin to work through our own inherited burden—through being present with ourselves and our own stories.

Why is the Pò important in this case?

It is because it is the spirit of instinctual practice brought to bear within the human body. It is an animalistic and, at times, an atavistic soul, possessed by each of us. If it is not protected it will lash out and may even work in such as a way that is deleterious to the person to whom it belongs.

It is also the spirit associated with justice, and at times, retribution.

The practices used in this case are manifold and will vary widely by tradition. They can include but are not limited to: participation in numinous events, such as prayer or scriptural participation, meditation, dance or other rhythmic encounter, conscious or semiconscious cohabitation of the body, herb and mineral medicines, override of the neural systems through pain or exercise (i.e., yoga, daoyin, yantra, etc.), and many others.

Engage in these as long as they are useful to you, and you are healthy enough to pursue them.

First, though, must come the awareness of what has been bestowed upon each of us.

What "lessons" were you "taught" that have been counter to your sense of serenity and openness to the world?

Reflect on the behaviors of the past, and find those times when you yourself might have affected others in the past.

Write these down.

Burn them to ash.

Rinse the ashes down and away with water. This can be done at any sink, toilet, or any semblance of an open drain. The ash can even be rinsed onto the ground to be absorbed, if no proper drain is available.

Talk to your Pò spirit; let that spirit of just behavior and uprightness be your confessor. If the Pò is healthy, that is.

Ask your Pò what it needs, what *you* need in order to be made whole. Ask it what behaviors you might change in order to address the burdens passed to you, and to prevent the inertia of your actions from being transmitted to others.

In all cases, the participant is asked to refine his or her consciousness, often by dissolving the bodily boundaries and moving into the deeper ancestral currents.

In the present work, the lower interior altar space, which resides in the area of the interior lumbar region is a space of the unknown, and, in a compromised state, great fear.

It is also the place of Fire within Water.

It is the abyss, and a place of the energy of the lineage of dead, both near and far in time, and, in the experience of the author is felt as a deep pull inward and down, to a point of coagulated tranquility. Even this stillness waits, as it is also the area from which the freed spark gives the first inkling of impetus. It is the place of black water gathered in a ravine, upon which the moon pierces white.

To Be Humane

Recognize in others the existence of inherited burden.

Do not be burdened with the burdens of others. Work to unburden yourself of what you have inherited. If you are able, contribute to the release of the burden of others.

If you find that you simply cannot divest yourself of what you have been given, work to transform it.

The goal in either case is to prevent your own burden from being passed on to others.

稚子气概

您是否尋求禮節？

Zhìzǐ Qìgài:

Nín shìfǒu xúnqiú lǐjié?

脆骨：

田鼠會找鷹嗎？

禮節是人民的工作，而不是一個人的工作。別人會告訴你禮節。

正直來自內部。

即將在天地之間找到和諧，通過人類的沉思精神表達出來。

這是直立的。

Cuìgú:

Tiánshǔ huì zhǎo yīng ma?

Lǐjié shì rénmín de gōngzuò, ér bùshì yīgèrén de gōngzuò. Biérén huì gàosù nǐ lǐjié.

Zhèngzhí láizì nèibù.

Jí jiàng zài tiāndì zhī jiān zhǎodào héxié, tōngguò rénlèi de chénsī jīngshén biǎodá chūlái.

Zhè shì zhǐlì de.

On Uprightness and Propriety

"Baby's Breath":

Do you know rén?

Do you know uprightness?

"Brittle Bones":

I know of it…

"Baby's Breath":

Do you seek propriety?

"Brittle Bones":

Does a vole seek a hawk?

Propriety is the work of the people, not of a person. Others will tell you of propriety.

Uprightness comes from within.

Set about to find accord between Heaven and Earth, expressed through the Shén spirits of humans.

This is upright.

Do not conflate propriety and uprightness.

The two are not always the same!

When you take from another to bolster yourself, this is not uprightness, even if the people say it is proper! In the same way, if one is crooked, one can still be upright.

One requires the permission of the people, the other requires the recognition of the spirits!

Know which of the two you are working from—and which you are working for.

COMMENTARY

UPRIGHTNESS IS CONDUCTING oneself in such a way that others around you will be better for your presence and in such a way that recognizes the light within another. It is generally the capacity for forthrightness in speech and action, as well as honesty, and a recognition and regard for others, even strangers. There is an openness which springs forth from this kind of approach and this allows for interconnectedness of persons.

Some will abjure you to recognize the inherent value of the being. Remember though that value is a human construct and is not really consistent across cultures.

Nearly all cultures will recognize the internal brightness of an individual which shines forth in the eyes and upon the face. There is the pull toward jian (見). This ensures that all are seen, recognized and acknowledged in a way that keeps the cohesion of the being.

In addition to being the spirit which animates the body and ensures vital movement, the Pò is also the spirit of justice and fairness. The extent to which it follows these is directly commensurate with the state of the Pò. If it has been wounded, insulted, or harmed, it will work with an eye toward revenge and retribution, or wrath. Conversely, if it is relatively healthy, or at least well supported, it will proceed in the name of restitution. The first approach generally requires some form of harm or loss to be visited upon the perpetrator of the insult. The second approach works to assure that one approaches some semblance of wholeness and restoration.

The Embodiment

Practice uprightness in relation to those around you as well as with yourself.

Strive to be constant in action, and consistent in your interactions with others. Work toward equanimity, and beware of having "favorites."

The uprightness,[55] or Yì (义), being spoken to in this passage is the capacity to treat oneself and others with fairness, equality, and the fundamental faithfulness of being, as well as a general conscientiousness.[56]

In this case, do not do unto others what you would not wish for yourself. If you wish cohesion and humane behavior to be directed toward you, do the same for others, but do not assume that what you find "good" will be viewed in the same light.

So-called "proper behavior" does not always meet this negative standard. Propriety is fine as long as it contributes to the being and does not take away from them something, which keeps them whole, coherent, and aware of the world around them.

If a standard based on awareness and cohesion is adopted, it also means that a "master" may not always have the right answer. Negotiate for yourself the level of involvement that you will have with propriety, but keep to the upright. Here too, recognize that upright may not be synonymous with the "straight and narrow" path. Human life is very often blurry, and one can appear crooked while maintaining uprightness. Work to maintain the values that are important to you which do not restrict the unfolding of life for another.

No one can do this for you.

To Be Humane

Enact benevolence and teach others to be upright in their comportment. Maintain your uprightness and practice integrity and coherence even when you are not being watched.

Always keep clear the distinction between propriety and uprightness. Practice both if they are in accord with one another, but hew to uprightness when they diverge. This maintains both your coherence and that of others.

---

55 David B. Schlosser, "The Five Virtues of Confucius": http://www.dbschlosser.com/five-virtues-of-confucius/ [Accessed on December 2, 2020].

56 There is also a sense of putting forth one's best effort imbedded in the Confucian interpretation of this virtue. Many Daoists would modify this definition to include doing what is the upmost of the natural function of a person. Also tied into this virtue is the idea of reciprocity and an altruistic consideration toward others.

稚子气概:

"君子是為了維護他的孤獨."

Zhìzǐ Qìgài:

"Jūnzǐ shì wèile wéihù tā de gūdú."

脆骨:

我的呼吸是我唯一會堅持的建議。

Cuìgú:

Wǒ de hūxī shì wǒ wéiyī huǐ jiānchí de jiànyì.

On Quietude and Solitude

"Baby's Breath":

In both the *Doctrine of the Mean* and in the *Great Learning*,[57] we are told: **"The jūnzǐ[58] is cautious of his solitude."[59]**

This is advice that we should all resolve to enact for ourselves, as it is in solitude that most of us are able to reach a state of clearness and awareness, both of ourselves and the world around us.

It is up to each of us what we should do with it.

"Brittle Bones":

My breath is the only counsel I will keep.

---

57 Both are considered to be representative works of the Neo-Confucian school.
58 The term Junzi (君子) is most commonly translated as "gentleman," and is used to indicate a refined person as well as one who is erudite and who has consideration for the larger social interconnections around him. While the term classically has male connotations, in contemporary usage, it is commonly used in the more neutral sense of "person."
59 Junzi shen qì du 君子慎其獨.

COMMENTARY

SOLITUDE IS THE space occupied by one. That is, to embody this, one need only to find the physical space to be alone with oneself. This is physical isolation from distraction, and difficult it is. Family requires our presence. Work requires our presence. We often require some form of "other" presence in the form of whatever is next, latest, greatest, or lost. Here, we are alone in a space with ourselves, but for the overriding presence of distraction. Solitude, however, is the presence of the body and mind in singular proximity. In solitude, we are not necessarily present.

This is the gift of quietude.

> How can one know the Dao? By the heart [Xīn].
> How can the heart [Xīn] know? By emptiness, the pure attention that unifies being and quietude...
> The heart [Xīn] is never without treasure...yet is is called empty...
> The heart [Xīn] is never not completely filled...yet it is called unified...
> The heart [Xīn] is never without movement...yet it is called quiet...[60]

The *Xunzi* asks us this central question and leaves it to each of us to search for an answer we already possess.

Quietude is the state of internal stillness, awareness, and presence within. Unlike solitude, it does not require the openness of space that can mark solitude. It is, rather, solitude within self.

This is the space wherein the chattering cacophony of the Mind slows. Thoughts come and are allowed to float away. Over time, the thoughts become less intense and less frequent.

JOHN ANDERSON

---

60 *Xunzi* Chapter 21, "Jiebi," in Claude Larre and Elisabeth Rochat de la Vallee (Trans.), *Rooted in Spirit: The Heart of Chinese Medicine* (Barrytown: Station Hill Press, 1995), 48.

As we are told, only calm water becomes clear. Further than this, it is only in still water that one can steal the light of the moon.

Quietude is a reflection of the Xīn, and does not require solitude in a physical sense, it only requires that we begin to let our thoughts sink away like sand sinking to the bottom of a pond.

The 16th chapter of the *Daodejing* advises one to move into quietude through the practice of solitude:

> Arrive at supreme emptiness Embrace deep silence
> Myriad creatures arise together I thereby observe them
> returning
> So many things blossoming
> And each returns back to its roots
> Returning to the roots is called silence
> This means returning to one's destiny-life-force (ming)
> Returning to one's destiny-life-force is called eternality
> Understanding eternality is called enlightenment

The jūnzǐ sees solitude as a means to an end and quietude as a returning to the path of the Ming. For some, solitude and quietude imply aloneness but not aloofness. The philosophical Daoist would likely have no qualms with either aloofness or involvement, but would use their own experience as the meter.

Even if we are unhappy with what we may find in this quietude (stillness) brought about through solitude (aloneness), it is ours nonetheless, and may unearth the many quiet talents which will encourage spontaneity and the irascible impediments which could keep us stone-still.

The Embodiment

As simple as the idea of this passage might be, it is paradoxically one of the most difficult for many of us to do. Solitude and quietude are free, but they must be found, and as found things, cannot be counted upon to appear with any regularity. It is incumbent, then, on each of us to find space in which quietude and solitude might appear, and one is easier to find than the other.

To practice this is easy enough in theory, but quite difficult to accomplish with regularity until much practice has been accrued.

The practice asks one to slow, and eventually stop thoughts from arising in the Mind.

So to begin, find those places that give the mind space to be silent. Find those places that put your mind at ease. To find that you are most quiet and tranquil at the beach, go to the beach. If it is a park, go there to be alone with yourself. This accomplishes the solitude often necessary when one first begins to work toward quietude.

Breathe in and out, in measured rhythms which can be maintained with ease.

In any situation, forget one position or state versus another as opposition.

Observe preferences in the Mind, and recognize the observation of those preferences. Think about your thinking.

Detach from this or that preference.

If you observe a thought happening or beginning to happen, recognize it and let it float away.

Return to the breath, and continue observing thoughts and letting them drift away.

Breathe in through the nose comfortably and rhythmically.

Observe the heartbeat.

This is perhaps the most important exercise for engaging your awareness of the Shén.

Listen to the rhythms of breath and heartbeat.

Feel the quality of the breath, and of the heartbeat.

Then let these impressions fall away.

This will slow the Shén and give it the openness necessary to take in experience.

The Shén is you, and you are it. When it slows, so do you.

To Be Humane

To be in quietude with oneself facilitates equanimity or evenness with others. The steadiness which quietude brings is at the heart of the virtue of Xīn.

And even solitude can be of use, as it is here, in solitude, when people most often recognize the need for others.

稚子气概：

保持內心開放就是讓道流向世界。

我們必須打開心臟/心靈的門戶以及身體的通過和通過。

Zhìzǐ Qìgài:

Bǎochí nèixīn kāifàng jiùshì ràng dào liúxiàng shìjiè.

Wǒmen bìxū dǎkāi xīnzàng/xīnlíng de ménhù yǐjí shēntǐ de tōngguò hé tōngguò.

脆骨：

如果我們要喝酒，葫蘆必須不開瓶

Cuìgú:

Rúguǒ wǒmen yào hējiǔ, húlu bìxū bù kāi píng.

On Opening the Heart

"Baby's Breath":

To keep the Heart open is to let the Dao flow into the world.

To have an openness of the Xīn is the beginning the of virtue, both as a power-of-being, and of Upright behavior.

It is the prerequisite for both.

We must open the portals of the Heart/Mind and the passes and throughways of the body.

We are hollow so that the Spirits can come to earth!

Openness is the vermillion spirit.

Which strives to join all things.

"Brittle Bones":

Another.

A gourd must be uncorked if we are to have spirits,

The Heart is the same.

COMMENTARY

THERE IS A saying in the Chinese culture:

鬼由心生.
GUǏ YÓU XĪN SHENG.
Devils [and ghosts] are born [nurtured and grown] in the heart.

That which is repressed begins to fester and rot. When one's experiences stagnate, they begin to darken the blood and cloud the spirits which rely on it. We become locked in by the gravity of our experience and have trouble finding grace from elsewhere.

In order for the diaphanous to shine through, the portals of the Heart must be open to receive it—if we could but open what has become stuck.

In the five-phase structure of embodied cosmology as it exists Chinese medicine and Chinese popular culture, the Heart is at once considered the most tender and also the most essential of the organs, and its resident spirit, the Shén, is considered to be primary within the complex of spirits which both inhabit the body and enliven and permit participation in existence as a whole.

As an addendum to the opening lines of this passage, one can also say following with certainty:

神心生.
SHÉN XĪN SHENG.
Spirits are born [nurtured and grown] in the heart.

This second phrase is the natural comportment of a Human being in both Daoism and Confucianism, and the key to this state of relationship with spirits and one's own native Shén is an "openness" of one's being.

Gǎntōng (感通), Rén (仁), and Relationship

The term "rén" (仁) as it has been most commonly used throughout this text implies the broader idea of humaneness. It has also translated as: "benevolence, love, altruism, kindness, charity, compassion, magnanimity, perfect virtue, goodness, true manhood, manhood at its best, human-heartedness, humanness, humanity, 'hominity,' man-to-manness" and "authoritative humanity."[61] All of these definitions square easily with the Confucian concept of rén. It is more difficult, however, to reconcile many of the Confucian virtues with Taoist tenants of personal ease and freedom of being. It is not impossible, though.

To the ancient Chinese mind, the dynamic concord of the cosmos relied on hidden spiritual forces that circulated through the interactions of human, divine, and natural beings. Accordingly, "gǎntōng" named the very manner in which sky and earth, the human and the divine, were brought together into a harmonious conjunction. It referred not only to the open comportment among persons, but also to the reciprocal intuition and communication between various animate forms in the human, spiritual, and natural worlds in general.[62] Here, it is important to note the root meaning of gǎntōng in the ancient Chinese mind: the intercourse of the primordial cosmic forces of yin and yang that were responsible for the birth and emergence of all beings in the universe.[63]

The concept of rén also has a connotation of communion, joining, and communication both with humans, nature, and other more subtle, unseen parts of existence.

---

61 The definitions of "benevolence," "love," "altruism," "kindness," "charity," "compassion," "magnanimity," "perfect virtue," "goodness," "true [humanhood]," "[humanhood]-at-its-best," "human-heartedness," "humanness," "humanity," "hominity," and "man-to-man-ness" attributed to Chen (1955). The gloss of Rén as "authoritative humanity" is attributed to Hall and Ames (1987), found in: Huang Huaiyu, "Rén and Gǎntōng: Openness of Heart and the Root of Confucianism," *Philosophy East & West* 62.4 (2012): 463–504.

62 See the "Xiuwen" (脩文) chapter of the Shuoyuan for further discussion on the development of moral cultivation as an agglutenating process from en 恩 (favor, kindness) to ai 愛 (love) to rén 仁 (humanness) and finally to ling 靈 (relationship to spiritual power and the spirits themselves).

63 Huang, "Rén and Gǎntōng," 465.

In ancient China we see the term "rén" used to denote a form of spiritual surrogacy wherein the kings of dynasties were also responsible for communing with the spirit world. The key to this communion was the openness of the heart "gǎntōng" which allowed this lived relationship to occur.[64]

In modern use, this term indicates a sense of familiarity with a thing, a connection which allows for relationship. Its use here tends to skew toward the realms of emotion and emotive process. It is therefore part and parcel of the lived human experience, and points to a personal "knowing" or engagement with self and others. This much is accurate, but given the brief discussion above, one can easily see how an "openness of the heart" extends far beyond the ideas of human affect or emotion—it indicates the state of being of both the qì as moving potential and potency and the Shén spirits.

To have the portals of the heart locked up tightly forestalls the proper movement of the qì and spirits into the Xīn and throughout the body. This in turn precludes open communication and the free expression of liveliness that is natural to the human experience.

There have been a number of states laid out above which indicate a lack of clear and proper function of the Xīn, or Heart-Mind, which is the psychological and spiritual outgrowth of the working of the Shén spirit, but there is a specific condition posited within the Shén-Hammer lineage of Chinese medicine which speaks specifically to a closing of the Xīn, or Heart.

Heart Closed[65]

Here, the capacity of the heart to except and interpret new experience is stifled because the heart is locked in such a way that new energy

JOHN ANDERSON

64 It also has the connotation of belonging, that like recognizes like and of "equals" joining. Here then, its meaning becomes quite personal in a manner which accepts the Confucian ideal, emphasizing a "higher" impulse toward humanity as a whole while also permitting and in the older usage of the term, even emphasizing specific respectful congress between individuals. Every sense of the term here requires that "openness" be present if the exchange is to have this parity of human equals.

65 See Leon Hammer, *Dragon Rises, Red Bird Flies: Psychology in Chinese Medicine* (New York: Eastland Press, 2005) for a more nuanced discussion of the causes and specific outcomes of Heart Closed.

cannot get in. This is likely caused when the insult takes place during a time when the individual is too weak or immature to defend itself or is insulted at a time when its psychological defenses are completely worn. Using the house metaphor, this would be the equivalent of shuttering the house, drawing the blinds, and locking the doors even though there is nothing inside. That this usually takes place at a younger age,[66] or at a time of specific vulnerability, implies that the individual raises this as a defense against the outside world. The net result is that new experience and the emotions which come with it are not allowed to be expressed in a full and natural way. This limits spontaneity, joy, and the feeling of connectedness with other human beings.

"...The gates of hell are locked on the inside."[67] To allow the torment and suffering to escape, there must first be an opening of the Heart, but this must first come from within, as well. Only once this takes place does the true nature of the personhood shine through with clarity and brightness.

In this sense, the doors to Heaven too, are locked on the inside.

In the Shen-Hammer lineage of Chinese medicine, there are several conditions which are apropos to this passage—specifically, "Heart Full," and "Heart Closed."[68] In their turn, each of these conditions can have a profound impact on the development of the individual, and can subsequently compromise any work toward adopting a more humane and human stance toward oneself and toward others which comes as a natural consequence of working with the singular Shén spirit of the Heart.

The Embodiment

When we talk about the Heart-mind, or Xīn, being "closed," we need to move away from the idea of the heart as metaphor. It is a vibrant,

---

66 Generally considered to be before 7 years of age, although the nature and degree of an insult, repetition of an insult, and constitutional composition of an individual can affect this.

67 C. S. Lewis, The Problem of Pain. (New York: Harper Collins, 2001), 626.

68 The clinical implications these conditions are explored in great detail within Dr. Hammer's *Dragon Rises, Red Bird Flies*.

pulsating system filled both with Love and Loss. These are two of the strongest components of the Humane experience. It is a space where energy should enter and leave freely. This is the flow of Yin and Yang between Heaven and Earth, embodied, and given over to a corporeal form, and it is no less than this.

In the same breath, any exercise that is undertaken to free the bound state of heart should be interpreted not as exercise in metaphor, but as literal forms of movement and opening and freedom which are vital to the proper function of the Xīn as an expression of the Heart-mind as the performative aspect of the Shén. This type of work is both experiential and existential in scope, and, in many cases, it can be both exorcistic and cathartic.

In the previous passage, we were warned that past experiences held within the heart will dictate, or at least color future experience. The heart needs to be open in order for experience to issue forth in a free, easy, spontaneous, and open sense.

The free-and-easy wanderer, both fool and sage, must have an open heart so that which is the basis of any experience can move through.

Start by listening for your own heartbeat.[69]

Go within the heart.

Pay attention to the rhythm of the heartbeat itself, taking care to count it in the chest, the head, the ears, the legs, the feet.[70]

Are some beats faster, slower, or even "heavier" or "lighter" than others?[71]

69 In modern societies, we must be careful not to reduce the Heart to its mere muscular structure, functioning only as a pump for the blood, beating with its everpresent rhythms, existing only for the circulation of the fluid medium. This mechanistic viewpoint is prevalent in more institutionalized forms of Chinese medicine. At the same time, we cannot be completely given over to seeing the heart structures as pure abstraction. This happens quite often and some "classical" forms of Chinese medicine and Daoist practice. On their own, neither of these is of much value for the work that is necessary for the reestablishment and continuance of the human way, such as it is entailed here.

70 If it is feasible and safe, draw a bath or use a hot tub in such a manner that you are lying face up in water that is warm enough to be comfortable, but not too hot, and with just enough depth to cover the ears to insulate them from outside noise. If the water is sufficiently warm, it will also accentuate the perception of the blood flow throughout the body. Barring that, use earplugs or even earbuds to block out as much background noise as is possible.

71 From a Western perspective, there will be some natural degree of heart rate variability (HRV) present within each of us. This is generally considered normal if it is not too pronounced. The Shen-Hammer lineage of pulse-diagnosis places great emphasis on the

Does your breathing affect the rhythm?

Next try to capture the physical sensation of the blood within the vessels as they pulse and move ever so gently.

On the whole, it should, like your breathing and the overall rhythm of the heartbeat itself, be smooth and steady. It should be relatively light in terms of pressure or "weight."

Notice this pressure or weight. Place your attention there.

Does it feel heavy, or tight, or even "full"?

Do you experience pressure from behind the sternum (the breast-bone), or a persistent heaviness in the chest, neck, over even the head?

Is there a sensation of heat?

Of cold?

Does your heart seem to "drop" on some beats? Perhaps there is even the feeling of a "ball" in the heart, similar to having a "lump in the throat."

All of these are physical sensations that are consistent with the "Heart-Closed" condition.

Is there a propensity for you to experience jealousy with those that you hold close? Or spite? These are emotional states correlating with the closing of the Heart.

To be clear, these emotional states may not be due to anything that you have done. Most of us would not choose to have a closed Heart in the face of the many trials and travails of human existence. It is, however, incumbent upon you to observe your own behaviors and reactions, and if warranted, to address them, if they are causing distress within your own life or others. In some cases, this might take the form of repeated meditation centered on the Heart itself. In other cases, help from an outside source may be necessary.

Work to open and purify the Heart so that that which shines though is itself diaphanous, smooth, and uncomplicated. This should be our countenance carried into the world.

The judicious use of an appropriate herbal formula is one of the strongest lines of engagement for this type of condition and an in-

---

rhythmicity of the heartbeat. It is true that the rhythm can be telling, particularly if entire beats are being missed, or half beats are being missed regularly. In this passage, it is the texture of the sensation on the heartbeat that is the main focus.

depth examination of a formula of the same name can give us valuable insight into the ways in which the human being can approach the process of restoration of the flow of qì and Shén within the heart.

HEART CLOSED FORMULA[72]

Chāngpú (*Acorus calamus.*; 菖蒲)
Opens the Orifices of the Heart (Xīn), transforms and disperses Phlegm, removes turbidity, calms the Spirit.

Chuānxiōng (*Ligustici Wallichii*; 川芎)
Invigorates the Blood and promotes the movement of qì.

Mùxiāng (*Costus Saussurea*; 木香)
Promotes movement of qì in the Middle Jiao.

Fúshén (*Poria Pararadicis*; 茯神)
Nourishes the Heart and calms the *Shén*

Yuǎnzhì (*Polygala Myrtifolia*; 遠志)
Calms the Spirit, sedates the Heart and clears the channel joining the Heart and Kidney

Suānzǎorén (*Zizyphi Spinosae*; 酸枣仁)
Nourishes Heart Yin and tonifies the Blood and calms the Spirit.

Yùjīn (*Curcumin*; 郁金)
Invigorates the Blood, dispels Blood Stasis, regulates qì flow.

Huánglián (*Coptis*; 黄连)
Clears Heart Fire. This often occurs when there is excess external stimulation, or when the Yang of the Middle or Lower Burners flares up. This is the interiorized equivalent of feeling agitated when you

JOHN ANDERSON

72 Leon Hammer and Hamilton Rotte, *Chinese Herbal Medicine: The Formulas of Dr. John H. F. Shen* (New York: Thieme, 2012).

are much too hot. This is the person with the red face and neck, who is quick to anger, who has high blood pressure, and who often feels hot.

Chénxiāng (*Aquilaria Agallocha*; 沉香)
Promotes movement of qì, specifically the descent of qì. This works to reestablish the Yang qì in the lower Jiao by directing it downward. This is the proper place of storage and emergence.

This formula is focused on opening up the portals of the Xīn. In contrast to the formula found in the next passage, it deals less with clearing dampness and phlegm, both obstructive in their own right to the internal space of the heart. In this passage, the door is locked, but the house is not full. It is much more focused on calming the heart and relaxing the tension found there.

Calming the Cinnabar Spirit Through Breath, Light, and Word

In the many extant Daoist traditions, there are several techniques meant to calm the Heart, ease the Mind, and safeguard the coming and going of the Shén spirits. Most common among them are techniques of breathing, intent, visualization, and intonation which serve to clear the qì of the Xin and calm the Shén.

The easiest, perhaps is the method used to move and cleanse the qì of the Xīn directly, although there is a correlate practice for each of the zàng organs which varies slightly for each organ. In this method, one visualizes inhaling a particular color of qì corresponding to the organ being cleansed. Upon exhalation, one is to visualize the turbid or impurity of that organ being exhaled along with the breath.

In this case, one visualizes the heart internally, observing what color shows there, and what feeling is present in the Xīn in the moment.

Inhale deeply through the nose imagining a vivid, pure, deep red light being inhaled with the breath. This red light is the appropriate visual component of the corresponding qì of the heart.

Let it circulate briefly and upon exhalation let any unclear, impure, or unwanted qì exit through the mouth with the breath. When exhaling, sub-vocalize a long sound similar to "Haaaaaah" or "Haaaaaaw" under the breath for the length of the exhalation.

Repeat this process several times, each time observing the "color" and texture of the Heat qì, and breathing out any qì which has become thick, unclear, constrained, or otherwise uncomfortable.

It is best to maintain a rhythm wherein the exhalation is at least twice the length of the inhalation. For example, one may inhale for three seconds, and exhale for at least six second.

This exercise serves to calm the Shén, or "Cinnabar Spirit" and to clear out any stagnant qì (particularly affects or emotions) which have settled there.

It is common during this exercise to have the felt-sense of pressure against the sternum from within. This is the process of the Xīn opening subtly. While this might be disconcerting at first, it can become quite softened by relaxing into the sensation.

The Daoist traditions also use mantras or invocations as another means by which to affect the purification, protection, and pacification of the Heart-mind and the Shén which reside there. Take the following:

净心神咒

JING XĪN SHEN ZHOU
Purifying the Heart Mantra[73]

---

73 http://fiveimmortals.com/the-eight-great-incantation/ [Accessed 12/4/2020]; A similar incantation is provided by Jerry Alan Johnson in *Daoist Magical Incantations, Hand Seals, and Star Stepping*, (Pacific Grove: The International Institute of Daoist Magic, 2006) as the "Purify the Heart and Spirit Incantation":

The Immortalized Laozi
Changes without stopping.
He removes the evil and keeps the good.
He protects my Destiny and my body.
Pure clarity and Wisdom
now comes from within me.
My Heart's spirit is calm and peaceful.
My three Hún are forever with me,
and my Pò are not dispersed.

We see Laozi, the legendary author of the Daodejing himself invoked as a benefic deity here.

JOHN ANDERSON

太上台星.

TAISHANG TAIXING.

Supreme Terraces of stars.

应变无停.

YINGBIAN WUTING.

Respond and transform without stopping.

驱邪缚魅.

QUXIE FUMEI.

Expel evil and restrain demons.

保命护身.

BAOMING HUSHEN.

Protect Life-Destiny and guard the body.

智慧明净.

ZHIHUI MINGJING.

Wisdom is bright and clear.

心神安宁.

XINSHEN ANNING.

The Heart Spirit is peaceful and tranquil.

三魂永久!

SANHÚN YONGJIU!

The Three Hún are everlasting!

魄无丧倾!

POWU SANGQIONG!

The [Pò] are not dying nor declining![74]

---

74 Other particularly sorcerous traditions of Daoism insert the line "Ji! Ji! Ru lu ling!" after this line. This is a common phrase used in Daoist magical workings which serves to impel either self or others to proper action or completion via the underlying authority of Heaven as embodied in the "Laws and Ordinances" of the celestial bureaucracy. This phrase serves as a driving force to the prayer which precedes it.

We find in this incantation one of the starting points both for broader forms of internal cultivation and for maintaining a clarity and verity of vision within the world.

Wang Fengyi gives us yet another meditative phrase to purify the Heart, this time with the Confucian emphasis on enacting and maintaining the virtues themselves. His affirmation of the Heart is this:

老善人看我明理？

LĂO SHÀNRÉN KÀN WǑ MÍNG LǏ?

Does Heaven see in me the quality of sacred connection?

我明理

WǑ MÍNG LǏ!

Yes! I have the quality of sacred connection![75]

This phrase was invoked as a countermeasure to hatred held within the Heart. The call-and-response format of this phrase provides the answer needed to affirm the depth of connection both with Heaven and with other people.[76]

There are, in these invocatory stanzas the beginnings of openness of the Heart, as purification is often one of the first steps, once the rhythm and cadence of the Heart and breath are recognized, to permitting freshness and newness to enter the portals and to abide with the Shén, and just as quickly to dismiss it. In this way, there is a fresh influx of being at every instant, and it must remain so if one is to maintain health, ease, and harmony.

Do bear in mind that the openness of the Heart spoken to here is not borne of metaphor. It is a literal, felt process, and if successful, working to open the Heart will produce a visceral response. You will feel it when openness does occur, and it may or may not be pleasant.

The state of the Heart—whether open or closed—speaks to the state of the mind, the body, and even the Spirit as literal points of ref-

75 Liu, *Let the Radiant Yang Shine Forth*, 277.

76 This emphasis on the interconnected nature of humanity is one of the characteristics which highlights the strong influence that Confucian ideas had on the teachings of Wang Fengyi, which were often referred to as Shan Rén Dao.

erence. In the Daoist tradition, the energetic constraints of a "closed" Heart have real-world consequences, which are imminent, palpable, and far reaching. The importance of this cannot be overstated.

To open the Xīn in the manner implied in the term gǎntōng (感通) is to allow the Shén to have the freedom to receive and experience existence. It is nothing less than this, and its importance cannot be understated.

To Be Humane

Openness of the Heart is perhaps simultaneously one of the most common tropes of human relationship and also the least practiced in any applied sense in the manner described above. We must learn to recognize, to work with, and to establish communication with our own Hearts and Spirits, if we are to meet others in the middle. Modern life attenuates the depth of communication and communion which mark a spirit-filled life. Life circumstance can further complicate connections with others. Even here, a choice must be made to connect if the Shén is to shine forth. Here, one becomes more human by beginning to recognize what is human within oneself.

This will allow us to receive others in all of their complexity and not be drowned in it.

There are times, though, when the Heart must be dredged out like a riverbed or mucked out like a horse stall. It will be unpleasant at first, but afterward will bring a lightness of person and a diaphaneity to being. This dovetails with the work detailed above, and is also the subject of the next section.

脆骨：

如果它是靈的祭壇，它應該是空的並且乾淨的。
如果您讓它裝滿了，而沒有匯款，那就繼續下
去…您會生病。

那些保持內心清晰的人可能會居住在那裡，但不
會永遠存在！

Cuìgú:

*Rúguǒ tā shì líng de jìtán, tā yīnggāi shì kōng de bìngqiě gānjìng de. Rúguǒ nín
ràng tā zhuāng mǎnle, ér méiyǒu huìkuǎn, nà jiù jìxù xiàqù...nín huì shēngbìng.*

*Nàxiē bǎochí nèixīn qīngxī de rén kěnéng huì jūzhù zài nàlǐ, dàn bù huì
yǒngyuǎn cúnzài!*

稚子气概：

心不會變，不能依靠讓舊的方式消亡。 在這種情
況下，僅存在沉氏住所。

...

這是氣和神的正常運動！

一個乾淨的房子可以接待客人！

Zhìzǐ Qìgài:

Xīn bù huì biàn, bùnéng yīkào ràng jiù de fāngshì xiāowáng. Zài zhè zhǒng qíngkuàng xià, jǐn cúnzài chén shì zhùsuǒ.

...

Zhè shì qì hé shén de zhèngcháng yùndòng!

Yīgè gānjìng de fáng zǐ kěyǐ jiēdài kèrén!

On Emptying the Heart

"Brittle Bones":

There are times when it is better to be alone than to suffer in the company of those who would take from you without your permission.

People will come into your presence and people will leave. This is the outcome of impermanence. Within the heart, there is no room for beggars!

If it is the altar of the spirit, it should be empty and clean. If you have let it fill, without remittance, carry on…you will become ill.

Those who keep the heart clear may reside there, but not forever!

Sometimes, old relationships become a form of waste which must needs be voided from the heart!

When it is healthy, the body knows when it needs to release waste. So, too, if it is healthy, the Heart-mind will do the same.

"Baby's Breath":

When two people are related to each other through jīng or through experience, there is play.

Each gives to the other.

It is the nature of the play which determines the quality of interrelatedness.

If both receive, there is accord. If not, there may be strife.

In either case, it is the Heart-mind which must endure the task!

The emotions connected to an unwanted relationship must be evacuated from the Heart just as material waste is voided from the bowels. Even here, the Pò reigns.

The Heart does naught and cannot be relied upon to let old ways die. In this case, the abode of the Shén only exists.

It simply will not do to ask a house to clean itself. It is through the stewardship of the Pò and the rhythm of the breath which it oversees which allows for this release of waste from the Heart.

This is the proper movement of qì and Shén!

A clear house is able to receive guests!

COMMENTARY

The heart must be empty if it is to receive. Under most circumstances the Heart keeps what is needed and only as long as needed. This applies to any aspect of existence to which the Heart and Shén spirit are extended. This constant and concurrent filling and emptying is what allows the spirits to shine through, and just as there is work to accepting change as it comes, by keeping the Xīn open (as above) and clear of the unwanted intrusions of the past which may repeatedly come to call.

If the Heart is over-full with painful, traumatic experience, it will repeatedly issue awareness only through the lens of this heavily laden experience. It changes the function of the Heart-mind and the spirits in a profound manner.

Heart Full

This is an energetic state in which there is qì trapped in the chest which cannot exit. The heart and the lungs bear the brunt of whatever insult caused the condition. Heart full can arise from many different causes which include, but are not limited to: psychological insult at an individual who is relatively robust and has reached some level of maturity both physically and psychologically (this allows for some degree of self-defense); physical trauma to the chest (such as might occur during a motor vehicle accident); and strenuous physical activity outside of the normal capacity of the individual.

What this amounts to is that whatever trauma occurred cannot be processed. The Heart remains filled with this stagnant qì. This precludes any new energy from entering into the system. This compromises the ability of the Shén to see clearly, and of the Pò to move, to digest, and to eventually integrate the myriad facets of human existence which encompass the physical, psychological, and even spiritual components of the human experience.

146

Again, this sort of experience not only serves to fracture the coherence of the heart, it also has the effect of compromising the ability of the Heart to take in new experience.

In addition, sometimes the energetic sequelæ of such unwanted experience can leave a palpable residue within the Heart-mind which further reinforce the reliving of the experience. In Chinese medicine this turbid, thick form of qì is referred to as "phlegm" and is not found in a healthy individual. This qì causes a muddying of perception and experience. Blurry eyes see blurry images and dirty windows show a dirty world.

The Embodiment

If the qì remains unmoved, there is a heaviness to one's bearing and a diminished capacity to recognize and interact with the world. This may result in changes in the senses, such as seeing or hearing stimuli which are not present in the external world. Often it is a sort of psychic filter—only permits some experiences while excluding or changing others, such as reliving a negative memory.

Sit with yourself to see what is in your Heart.

Do you revisit the same moments of your life hoping for a different outcome?

Are there conversations that you have out loud that are won by you in hindsight, given a different response?

Does the body freeze up or flare up with a smoldering rage when a certain memory comes to the surface, or when conditions are similar to it?

Do they trap the breath?

Recognize these!

Give them a voice.

Write them down.

It may be useful to take an herbal formula meant to break apart and move obstruction in the Xīn:

Chāngpú (*Acorus calamus*; 菖蒲)
Opens the Orifices of the Heart (Xīn), transforms and disperses Phlegm, removes turbidity, calms the Spirit.

Chuānxiōng (*Ligustici Wallichii*; 川芎)
Invigorates the Blood and promotes the movement of qì.

Yuǎnzhì (*Polygala Myrtifolia*; 遠志)
Calms the Spirit, sedates the Heart and clears the channel joining the Heart and Kidney

Yùjīn (*Curcumin*; 郁金)
Invigorates the Blood, dispels Blood Stasis, regulates qì flow.

Huánglián (*Coptis*; 黄连)
Clears Heart Fire. This often occurs when there is excess external stimulation, or when the Yang of the Middle or Lower Burners flares up. This is the interiorized equivalent of feeling agitated when you are much too hot. This is the person with the red face and neck, who is quick to anger, who has high blood pressure, and who often feels hot.

Chénxiāng (*Aquilaria Agallocha*; 沉香)
Promotes movement of qì, specifically the descent of qì. This works to reestablish the Yang qì in the lower Jiao by directing it downward. This is the proper place of storage and emergence.

Fúlíng (*Cocos Poria*; 茯苓)
Quiets the Heart, calms the Spirit and soothes the nerves. Also serves to remove Dampness[78] which can cause sluggishness and can contribute to the generation of phlegm.

77 Hammer and Rotte, *Chinese Herbal Medicine*, 9.
78 "Dampness" is a term used in Chinese medicine to denote a state of qì which is most commonly caused by digestive deficiniency and which often manifests physically as bloating, fatigue, and in some cases, minor retention of fluids. In the present context,

Huángqín (*Scutellaria baicalensis*: 黄芩)
Assists the Yang in descending to the Lower Jiao. Serves to clear heat so as to reduce agitation.

Báisháo (*Paeoniae alba*; 白芍)
Calms and descends the Yang. Helps to modulate and balance the Yingqi and Weiqi (i.e., the nutritive (inner) and defensive (outer) qì).

The primary emphasis of this herbal formula is to reduce the thickened qì preventing the opening of the Heart, just as above, and also to soften qì which has become recalcitrant, and to more vigorously move the qì (in this case, usually emotions, but can also be functional qì which keeps the Heart beating) that has become "stuck" in the Heart so that it can exit, thus reestablishing the fertile emptiness which is natural to the Xīn.

Lastly, one can use any of the techniques mentioned in the previous passage to help encourage the movement of "stuck" qì, which might be impeding change in one's life.

In all, we must learn to awaken the Xīn and keep it clear while we nourish it.

* * *
* *
*

however, it is more appropriate to recognize the idea of "Dampness" as being more akin to a "dampening of qì" through restriction by diminution, rather than as a literal indicator of the state of fluid metabolism within the body. Both readings are in line with the principles of Chinese medicine.

To Be Humane

To hold a great burden in the heart precludes experience and affects the ability to hold space for another. The experience of the "other" becomes self-referential for one whose Heart is full and unduly over-burdened.

To clear the Heart, then, is to regain the capacity to be fully present with another being. The awareness is freed, and the moment-in-itself can unfold naturally.

It is through the movement of the Xīn that the Shén of two individuals can "meet." This is seen in the clarity of the eyes and the resonance and timbre of the voice, but the Shén "know" even before this, and can interact before we are conscious of it.

稚子气概：

用服務標記您的時間！

這是提供給您周圍其他人的服務。

這是配發的適當用途之一。

您付出的犧牲不是流血的，也不是物體的。 這是一個人一生分配的一部分，以便他人能夠實現自己的自發性以體現道。

Zhìzǐ Qìgài:

Yòng fúwù biāojì nín de shíjiān!

Zhè shì tígōng jǐ nín zhōuwéi qítārén de fúwù.

Zhè shì pèi fā de shìdàng yòngtú zhī yī.

Nín fùchū de xīshēng bùshì liúxuè de, yě bùshì wùtǐ de. Zhè shì yīgèrén yīshēng fēnpèi de yībùfèn, yǐbiàn tā rén nénggòu shíxiàn zìjǐ de zìfā xìng yǐ tǐxiàn dào.

脆骨：

即使正統的做法毀了它，眾神仍然想要獻上鮮血，肉體和命運，並且他們仍然接受它們。

如何實現的？

通過人類的儀式工作。

成為人類，就是天地之間的橋樑。

Cuìgú:

Jíshǐ zhèngtǒng de zuòfǎ huǐle tā, zhòng shén réngrán xiǎng yào xiàn shàng xiānxiě, ròutǐ hé mìngyùn, bìngqiě tāmen réngrán jiēshòu tāmen.

Rúhé shíxiàn de?

Tōngguò rénlèi de yíshì gōngzuò.

Chéngwéi rénlèi, jiùshì tiāndì zhī jiān de qiáoliáng.

On Rendering Sacrifice

"Baby's Breath":

In ancient times, the people gave sacrifice to the gods.

The vessels of bronze and wood were filled with food and wine, which the living would only partake of once the spirits had had their share.

They blessed the offering by consuming it.

The altars were covered with cloth and woods of cinnamon, sandalwood, and camphor.

Meat, rice, and millet, fruit, water and wine, which all provided the substantiation of the gods and other spirits.

This was considered the proper way to show reverence—this is the core of li, the virtue of ritual practice.

Sacrifice marked the calendar.

Mark your time with service!

This is service rendered to others around you.

This is one of the proper uses of one's allotment.

The sacrifice you give is not of blood or of object. It is the giving of part of one's allotment of life-time, so that others will be able to realize spontaneity in themselves in order to embody the Dao.

"Brittle Bones":

The Orthodox followers of the Dao do not let that which is unclean lay next to that which is clean in some rites.

The sacred and the profane do not coexist on the altars to the "High" gods.

Let us remember, though that, in the past, even the "High" gods desired blood, flesh, and bone so that they themselves could come into this world, quickened, and robed in the very same.

Never forget this!

Even as the orthodox practices decry it, the gods still want tributes of blood, flesh, and destiny, and they still receive them.

How is this achieved?

Through the ritual work of humans.

To be human is to be the bridge between Heaven and Earth.

"Baby's Breath":

Let your sacrifice be you. But let your sacrifice to the gods be given as service to those around you who ask for it.

Let your service be your ritual, and let your ritual be your service rendered.

"Brittle Bones":

If one proceeds in this manner, "sacred" and "profane" dissolve, and one is left only with doing and not-doing.

COMMENTARY

DURING THE SHANG dynasty, sacrifice was all the rage. We can still find in museums and at archeological excavations, vessels of bronze, ritual implements used to transmogrify food and fluid into the otherworldly essences which the spirits of the gods and ancestors could ingest and entertain—such as they were capable, anyway.[79]

Various substances of sacrifice were proffered to the denizens of the spirit world during this time period, with rice and millet being commonly used grains, and deer and sheep used as flesh, both of which were intended to curry or maintain the favor of the gods and other spirits.[80]

Even to the present day, long lists of sacrificial substances can be found in the collected written corpus of the Daoist religion. Sheep, pig, and goat are still used in rituals, although these "bloody" materials are reserved for lower level gods or earth-bound spirits, such as hungry ghosts and spirits orphaned by lack of ritual propitiation. So, too, rice and millet are still found on Daoist altars alongside wine, liquors, water, and various objects needed for writing and recordkeeping in the Heavenly halls.[81] In all of these cases, the substance or item takes a position of primary importance, with omissions or mistakes being punishable by the gods and spirits.

The nature, timing, and importance of sacrifice is subject to change over time with some substances either coming into vogue or becoming outdated, at best, and at worst, taboo.

From the perspective of the present reading of Daoist lay practice, the most finite resource we possess is our allotted Ming, or destiny, which is experiential component of our lives. If you are to live the

---

79 David Keightley and Henry Rosemont, *These Bones Shall Rise Again: Selected Writings on Early China* (Albany: SUNY Press, 2014).

80 See Keightley and Rosemont above as well as Sarah Allan, *The Shape of the Turtle: Myth, Art and Cosmos in Early China* (Albany: SUNY Press, 1991) for a deeper reading of the role of sacrifice in ancient China.

81 Livia Kohn and Harold. D. Roth, *Daoist Identity: History, Lineage, and Ritual.* (Honolulu: University of Hawaii Press, 2002).

Dao, and to inculcate it in others, then experience must be dedicated to others for the sake of spreading spontaneity and growth as one would spread seeds. In some cases, you may tend the seeds to ensure that they take hold and grow. This is cultivation of self and other. In other cases, you may let the seed root and grow of its own accord. In either case, there must be a fertile ground, and this must itself be tended to regularly.

The Embodiment

To this end, share your experience, your "time," and your expertise with others. Do so for free, if you wish. Do so for compensation, if you wish. Invest your allotment, but do so sincerely and for the love of the shared experience.

Volunteer to help others who do not have the resources or knowledge. This may be something as "simple" as volunteering to feed those in need or answering an information hotline, or it could entail work with more profound existential outcomes, such as might be needed to fight fires, or to help others pass on peacefully.

Teach others a skill or discipline which brings some sense of contentment, creativity, or quiet to the world. This is one of the deepest ways in which your experience can be shared. Doing this, your Ming is both shared with others, and is given even greater depth. In addition, you also begin to expand and deepen the Ming of the people you teach.

If you are to teach, there are two things to consider about the act itself.

First, if you are teaching others in order to provide a scaffold upon which they will build, teach thoroughly so that the skills and knowledge are forthcoming and clear. This may require more or less work for individual students, and you, giving your experience will come to recognize what is needed.

Second, if the framework of knowledge is present, give the student only as much as is needed to foster their own growth and cultivation. Let them earn what they know and encourage them for it.

Be mindful so as not to spoon feed knowledge to a student, colleague, or friend if they are capable of the discernment for themselves. Let each arrive at his or her place through the work that each puts forth, giving to each what is necessary for the lesson to be learned and the beginning of the next lesson to arise. To do otherwise is to stifle the creative impulse.

Instill in everyone you meet a sense of curiosity and wonder. Humans naturally wish to share experience with one another, and the willingness to share knowledge, expertise, or even a listening ear allows one to participate more fully in the human realm, and a chance to be more human in the process.

Acknowledgement should be given at this point to the role that rendering of service, or even of sacrifice, of ourselves, to others can play for those neglected parts of our own being. It is important to know what we can afford to "give" ourselves, and, in light of this, still render service to others.

Take care not to let this turn into intractable egoism. Giving of oneself and sacrificing yourself loudly are very different things. Let appreciation be and appreciate yourself for the experience of giving unto others.

Take care of yourself so that you can take care of others, even if only by virtue of your existence. This service-to-oneself lies first in the recognition of what one deeply needs.

To Be Humane

To have "rén"—that most Confucian of virtues—is to have a focus toward humanity as a whole, and the giving of oneself to one person in the manner described here is the giving from oneself to all of humanity as it has a distinct tendency to multiply. If it is done freely and openly, this type of self-sacrifice is as humane as one can be, but never forget Humaneness for yourself.

稚子气概：

改變生活的不是痛苦，

痛苦做到了。

在很大程度上，痛苦是不可避免的，但遭受痛苦
是體驗中最棘手的部分。

Zhìzǐ Qìgài:

Gǎibiàn shēnghuó de bùshì tòngkǔ,

tòngkǔ zuò dàole.

Zài hěn dà chéngdù shàng, tòngkǔ shì bùkě bìmiǎn de, dàn zāoshòu tòngkǔ shì tǐyàn zhōng zuì jíshǒu de bùfèn.

脆骨：

即使您必須忍受生活帶來的痛苦，也沒有遭受痛
苦的偏愛，

讓苦難成為一個路標，然後無視這個標誌！

這就是方法。

Cuìgú:

Jíshǐ nín bìxū rěnshòu shēnghuó dài lái de tòngkǔ, yě méiyǒu zāoshòu tòngkǔ de piān'ài,

ràng kǔnàn chéngwéi yīgè lùbiāo, ránhòu wúshì zhège biāozhì!

Zhè jiùshì fāngfǎ.

On Suffering

"Baby's Breath":

Martyrs are not made at the pulpit.

They are made at the tip of the spear,

the loop of the noose, or the crushing heaviness of stone and earth.

To have pain is part of life.

It can be a boon or a scourge.

The suffering brought on is different.

It is not the pain which changes a life,

Suffering does this.

Largely, pain is unavoidable, but suffering from it is the trickiest part of the experience.

Much of suffering can be changed.

"Brittle Bones":

There is no weakness in pain, on its own. There is no weakness in suffering, in itself.

What to do?

The use of pain to transform suffering is fine, for this is embracing what is.

Have no preference for suffering, even as you must endure the pain which accompanies living,

Let suffering be a signpost, then disregard the sign!

This is the Way.

COMMENTARY

THERE IS ONLY so much that you can do to address pain—either physical, psychological, or otherwise. At times is best to do nothing but hold space for the individual who is in pain, including yourself. Sometimes it is all that can be done.

Pain is the sensation of discomfort found in the body, the Mind, and the spirit. Suffering is the aftermath of this feeling. It is a quality which very often stops us in our tracks and changes our relationship to our lives and to the time constituted by the rhythms of the body and the breath. It is suffering that determines whether we will leave the bed to shower when we are depressed, while the pain we feel internally is the manifestation of depression, most directly.

From the Daoist perspective, it is often counterproductive to blunt all of the pain that one feels. Indeed, many times we should work to actively feel what we are feeling, even if this is painful.

As Jung says: "...there is no coming to consciousness without pain."[82]

There is, in this, an acknowledgement of one of the "gifts" of pain, and this as a means to compassion as a stance.

Compassion

Compassion is something most traditions would encourage, but many people either do not have a deep experience of this emotion, or they may have difficulty articulating it, even if it is widely considered a desirable trait and a noble undertaking. As with unbidden emotions, one must learn to connect with the more virtuous emotions and the actions which proceed from them.

In many cases, we must rely on an initial stand-in as we begin to recognize, acknowledge, and explore the complexities of nascent

---

82 C. G. Jung, *Contributions to Analytical Psychology* (Abington: Routledge & Kegan Paul, 1948), 193.

JOHN ANDERSON

psychic and emotional materials, to which we are so often painfully prone. Figures and icons are set to do this on more than one level. First, these items tend to provide a raw embodiment, an open physicality and firmness, for the spirits which might reside within them. Thus, they can become an intermediary between ourselves and the many invisible worlds underpinning the cosmologies of many of the world's cultures. This is vital for the well-being of individuals participating in these cultural milieus. In addition, they can provide a quiet proxy, while the person learns to recognize internal states in order to harness or release them.

Externally, Kali is a killer, a wrathful being, often called upon in the West to protect and avenge.[83] When we interact with her on a physical level or with depth, we are given a chance to recognize and acknowledge our own sense of anger or wrath as we work into the places where insult lies. A statue provides us with the raw physicality emblazoned in space to encounter the thing as external or other to us, which often then makes the material "safer" or more comfortable for us to approach, experience, and move.

The Weeping Buddha or the Crying Mary are said to grant compassion and strength in times of pain and adversity. Certainly, they can provide a space in which one can let these entities take on or take in the emotions that we feel, particularly if they are uncomfortable or unfamiliar to us. Sadness, grief, and loss are the most common emotions with which they tend to be approached, and both entities can be useful in allowing one to let those feelings be expressed. They can also provide a means for experiencing compassion. In the case of the weeping form of the Buddha, one is instructed to rub His back as a means of comforting Being who regrets our own inevitable suffering, until we are able to move through and past the dukka (suffering). In the case of the dolorosa aspect of Mary, we find customs of cleaning, anointing, and even feeding. Both of these forms of Mary and Buddha

---

83 This is accurate in an external sense, but it must be emphasized that in addition to her ability to destroy others, as seen in her slaying of Shiva, her creative counterpart, that She also beheads herself to illustrate the illusory nature of wrath and the impermanent nature of even her own being.

ask us to transform sadness over our own personal circumstances into compassion for the many, indeed, all of creation.

The Embodiment

Sit with your pain and discomfort.

Sit with your suffering.

Realize that the two are not the same. Pain does not always bring with it suffering, but suffering always brings pain, even if the pain isn't physical.[84]

When pain or discomfort comes, breathe into it, breathe through it.

Do these play a role for you, and can you utilize, for yourself or for others, the qì inherent in this pain or suffering?[85]

Within this passage, there is also the innate recognition that both pain and suffering are impermanent, and further that both are subject to change.

Contemplate what this might mean for you.

Do you cling to the experience of pain? Of suffering?

What do you do to relieve the pain? How do you address your suffering as an individual?

Meditation for Compassion

The most prevalent form of practice here in modern use is the "metta" form of meditation that encourages "loving-kindness" toward others. In this form of meditation, one is asked to call forth feelings of love and kindness toward all beings in the following manner:

- Those we already love.
- Those to whom we are well disposed.
- Those to whom we feel neutral.
- Those to whom we are not well-disposed.
- Those who we actively dislike.

JOHN ANDERSON

84 Anguish and dread are forms of "pain," in a manner of speaking.
85 A great many people are able to direct their experiences of pain or suffering. There has been a vast amount of art in various forms which was and is borne on the back of pain and suffering.

To Be Humane

The humaneness inherent in pain and suffering is the realization of its universality and the upwelling of compassion toward one's fellow beings in the face of suffering.

This, on its own, can be difficult enough, and all the more difficult if we have not practiced compassion for ourselves in the face of our own suffering.

脆骨：

我會投我自己的肋骨知道神，誰的上升和下降以
自己的方式命運。

我將使用自己的肩骨來預言神諭。

閱讀皮膚上的裂縫，您將了解自己的未來。

Cuìgú:

Wǒ huì tóu wǒ zìjǐ de lèigǔ zhīdào shén, shuí de shàngshēng hé xiàjiàng yǐ zìjǐ de fāngshì mìngyùn.

Wǒ jiāng shǐyòng zìjǐ de jiān gǔ lái yùyán shén yù.

Yuèdú pífū shàng de lièfèng, nín jiāng liǎojiě zìjǐ de wèilái.

稚子气概：

身體提供了該死的理由和救贖的手段。

但是，任何一個都不比另一個真實。

Zhìzǐ Qìgài:

Shēntǐ tígōngle gāisǐ de lǐyóu hé jiùshú de shǒuduàn.

Dànshì, rènhé yīgè dōu bùbǐ lìng yīgè zhēnshí.

脆骨：

即使我很脆，我也是粹.

Cuìgú:

Jíshǐ wǒ hěn cuì, wǒ yěshì cuì.

稚子气概：

身體是通過妊娠和分娩獲得的。

什麼聖人是先要吮吸和接受，而後才學會咀嚼的聖人呢？

Zhìzǐ Qìgài:

Shēntǐ shì tōngguò rènshēn hé fēnmiǎn huòdé de.

Shénme shèngrén shì xiān yào shǔnxī hé jiēshòu, érhòu cái xuéhuì jǔjué de shèngrén ne?

On the Body

"Brittle Bones":

Old Tree tells us: It is because I am useless that I am not used. I do what needs to be done and only this.

I will cast my own ribs to know the fate of the Gods, who rise and fall in their own ways.

I will put fire to my own shoulder blades to divine the oracle.

Read the cracks and lines on your skin and you will know your future.

"Baby's Breath:

The body provides the reason for damnation and the means toward salvation.

But neither is more or less real than the other.

The Mind, Hùndùn!

The Body, Hùndùn!

Both are contained Chaos.

We may yet all be butterflies,

Or oxen.

"Brittle Bones":

Whatever those strange things mean to you, my companion may be right.

Even as I am cuì (脆), I am cuì (粹).

Immortality is fine.

But you still transform while sitting on a rock

"Baby's Breath":

A body is given through gestation and birth.

What sage is a sage who didn't first have to suckle and receive, only later learning to chew through?

Wisdom comes from gnawing the gristle life so generously provides.

Knowing that this is still food.

In this way, one can be both brittle and pure.

COMMENTARY

LÉIGŌNG (雷公), the "Thunder General," "Thunder Sire," or "Thunder God," is commonly encountered in acts of protection, empowerment, and even exorcism up to the present day. He is considered one of the deities *par excellence* for getting things done in an expedient and decisive manner. Incense, libations, and food all populate altars dedicated to him across the Asian world. How he is called, and what it means when he arrives however differ vastly depending on context across time. Some of the earliest representations of Léigōng portray him as a violent, nearly bumbling character who was revered in local cults around areas of southern China.

> While the earliest references around the Han dynasty (206 BCE–220 CE) tend to imagine Thunder either as a dragon or as a muscleman called "Sire Thunder," later sources visualize him in a variety of manifestations, most famously as an ugly bird-man hybrid, a pig with a pointy snout, or a monkey with an eminently protruding mandible (52).[86]

These representations are externalized and wild, not yet fully under the control of any sense of organizing principle. Over time, however, we find that this view of Léigōng had changed to fit the culture of spiritual control

> [T]he T'ang records concretely mark Sire Thunder's transformation from local oddity into supra-regional agent of a Daoist ritual vision. Crucially, this transformation is closely linked to his subjugation within ritual procedures for summoning Thunder by means of formal registration. Quite literally so, as many Tang tales recount encounters with Sire Thunder that

JOHN ANDERSON

86 Mark Meulenbeld, "Daoist Modes of Perception: 'Registering' the Living Manifestations of Sire Thunder, and Why Zhuang Zi is Relevant," *Daoism: Religion, History and Society* 8 (2016): 35–91.

lead to the process of having him depicted, iconized, or otherwise "formalized" in talismanic shapes.[87]

By this time, the spirit became "codified" in form and function as well as in method (i.e., the structures and techniques used to call Léigōng as a separate entity).

In yet another change in being, Léigōng becomes an entity whose existence is most fully actualized within the body of an adept as a co-creatrix and initiator. This implies that the body is given over, at least in part, to the righteous and upright Yang of Heaven.

The collective Shén are no different in this respect than the Thunder Sire, and there is a natural move toward physicality or localization within certain strata of the body. Incarnation is essential to the enactment of the tianli, the natural order of things, which begins with the movement of the spirits, and the human body is naturally attuned to the workings of the Hún, the Shén, and the Pò as relatively active and independent structures of the self and which have lighter or denser natures. Broadly the Hún ("Cloud Souls") and the Pò ("Bone Souls") exist in a dynamic state of existential opposition to one another while the Shén spirit mediates the constant push-pull between them.[88]

Our ability to work with the body is intimately interwoven with the way in which we see reality, and like Léigōng, how we go into the world, how we manifest, largely depends on the way in which we are viewed and how we view ourselves as a composite whole.

In this sense, the body of the individual more closely resembles a "body of work"[89] than a distinct entity moving through an "exter-

---

87 Meulenbeld, "Daoist Modes," 52–53.

88 As one might imagine these two types of spirits, while native to each of us, may not always be in accordance with one another within us:

"The [three] Hún fill the role of director-spirits. Enjoying freedom of movement, they leave the body during sleep or trance...[T]hey go to Heaven at certain times to report on a person's activities; but they are just and only accuse their host in the case of serious sins...The [seven] Pò on the contrary deliberately aim to destroy us. They are the spirits of the skeleton, that which is heaviest in the human body, most earthbound." (Schipperer, *The Taoist Body*, 36.)

89 In the same way that an artist or a musician creates and adds to a catalogue of work using intertwined or emblematic themes as well as repeated visual or auditory motifs, the individual does the same by using the (mostly) local body as a tool to fulfill its "catalogue" expressed by the term Ming.

nal" world. At times, the work is the work of the person as a whole. At times it is work performed on behalf of the individual, at times the "work" is the unwelcome encroach of life experience.

We must naturally work through a change from viewing the body as an unruly other to perceiving it as a familiar tool to be manipulated to a deep abiding within—we are thus each like Léigōng. The key to this change lies in understanding the viscera of the body, which exist in a manner similar to the visible tip of an iceberg.

This section emphasizes the zàng (solid) organs, as they are the primary philosophical focus of the body within major, contemporary currents of Chinese popular culture. The viscera are not only the physicality—the Incorporated seats the Shén—capable of holding, protecting, housing, and rooting them so as to keep them still and supple, but the viscera are also the natural physical consequence of the Shén Spirits themselves unfolding, emanating, and functioning in accordance with the cosmic order or law as received from heaven (Tiānlǐ; 天理[90]). That is, the zàng organs are the main points of embodied contact between heaven and human, and some of the strongest and strangest means of influence for the spirits upon the physical world. The movement of the spirits is delineated and realized at its most basic level by the smooth functioning of the zàng organs themselves, which help to assure the unfolding of the totality of an incarnated life.

Each of the five Shén is housed within one of the five zàng organs which grow from infancy, flourish during the life cycle, and eventually begin to weaken and wither as the result of circumstance, choice, and the persistence of embodied time.

The correspondence between the Shén spirits and the five zàng organs[91] is as follows:

The Heart pertains to the Fire Phase, is controlled by, and is the seat of the singular Shén spirit.

JOHN ANDERSON

90 The meaning of this term is more akin to the concept of "the natural order of things" than a discreet proscriptive mandate.

91 There is a sixth organ (and corresponding spirit), which is sometimes included in discussions of the body, that being the gallbladder. In many cases, its function and resident spirit are subsumed under the Wood phase and therefore its function is often attributed to the aegis of the Hún/Liver.

The Spleen pertains to the Earth Phase, is controlled by, and is the seat of the Yì. It allows for the synthesis and distribution of nutritional resources. To deplete it is to deplete the material component of the post-Heaven or post-natal qì.

The Lungs pertain to the Metal Phase, are controlled by, and are the seat of the Pò soul.

The Kidneys pertain to the Water Phase, are controlled by, and are the seat of the Zhì (the "Will"). Extreme overwork ("burning the candle at both ends") depletes the Kidney qì. To deplete the pre-Heaven or pre-natal qì held within the Kidneys is to shorten one's life.[92] The Liver pertains to the Wood Phase, is controlled by, and is the seat of the Hún soul. To deplete the Liver is to deplete the Blood stored within it. This affects one's vision.

Furthermore, each of the organs pertains to one or more bodily tissues or substances whose abundance and vitality coincide with the proper function of the organ. Lastly, each of these organs is said to "open" or manifest in the function of each of the sense organs.

In this case:

The Heart pertains to the vessels. It therefore governs the blood vessels, and circulation of blood. It "opens" to the tongue.

The Spleen pertains to the muscles. It governs bodily mass, form, and physical capacity. It "opens" to the lips/exterior mouth.

The Lungs pertain to the skin and body hair. It governs texture and composition of skin and mucus membranes. It "opens" to the nose.

The Kidneys pertain to the bones. (and Marrow). They "open" to the ears.

The Liver pertains to the tendons (i.e., connective tissue). It "opens" to the eyes.

In contrast to the organ-centered approach laid out in the *Huangdi Neijing* and other classics of the Han dynasty, the present work places emphasis on the primacy of the spirit in the process of incarnation with the physicality of the organ existing as a natural, if necessary, outgrowth of these Spirits and souls which work together within an

92 Unschuld, *Huang Di nei jing su wen*.

individual. Admittedly, this animistic approach is at odds with modern interpretations, which place such solid emphasis on the the physicality of the organs, while often paying begrudging lip service to the more invisible elements of the person.[93]

The upshot of the approach taken in this text is that it not only puts the spirits in contact with the zàng organs which house them, but it also acknowledges the link between the spirits and specific tissues themselves, and that, furthermore, the function of the tissue falls under the ægis of the working capacity of the individual Shén spirits.

Within Daoist metaphysics, the body is a necessity to experience life as we find it. The body is not seen as a burden *a priori*, as it is within so many other traditions, but it can *become* a burden as the result of our own actions in the face of life experience. The nineteenth-century peasant-saint Wang Fengyi states:

> The Body is that aspect of us that responds to the material world. If there are jobs here [in the world] that you don't know how to do, just study them with earnest effort. The more you do them, the more strength you will have; the more you study them, the more progress you will make.[94]

Rather than denying importance of the body, one is encouraged herein to use it, even to revel in it, to a point, in order that one might better understand the world. This applies not only to the material world and one's being therein, but also the more "spiritual" aspects of experience.

In addition, many forms of Daoist practice center around installing or seating one or several spirits within the body which are not altogether native to the human being. Some of the more common ex-

93 This approach, which can be readily encountered in the modern milieu of Chinese medicine can border on materialism. This is particularly evident in the codified approach to Chinese medicine propagated after the Chinese Cultural Revolution. In this case, much of what might be considered "traditional" or "indigenous" was stripped away from the medicine (and the culture at large) in lieu of a contemporary Western scientific approach and a further adoption of Western cultural norms already underway for many decades before Mao Zidong rose to power.

94 Wang Fengyi, *Twelve Characters: A Transmission of Wang Fengyi's Teachings*, translated by Sabine Wilms, (Corbett: Happy Goat, 2014), 21.

amples of this in religious Daoism include the General or Duke of Thunder (Léigōng) or, as in the Shangqing tradition, the Three Pure Ones.

Even familiar forms of ritual make use of the body as a beginning point. The "mundane" use of prayer beads in a great many traditions illustrates this and is just one specific example of embodied process. The counting of prayers is done through the running of the beads through the hands or fingers. Prayers worked thusly have an embodied component that relies upon the presence and engagement with a corporeal form. Singing, dancing, chanting, posture, and externalized ritual are all used to purify the body, or even to render the body sacredote to some extent by dent of its participation in and with the sacred.

In many of the Daoist traditions, the body is not the starting point, but a necessary component of other, more subtle acts which, while not necessarily a goal for many of us, are also not altogether alien to us. That is, our corporeality allows us access to more than overt sensory perception, and our internal sensorium, while often self-referent in our day-to-day existence is also able to pick up on other beings which may be pertinent to us. Baker writes:

> At the same time the [adept] enters his internal, embodied subjectivity, the potential for other, disembodied subjectivities arises. Ghosts and spirits are thus reflections of the interior self that is accessed through, but which somehow transcends corporeal awareness. The simultaneous awareness of one's interior being and of the presence of ghosts and spirits suggests that both are part of the same processes of bodily consciousness.[95]

A body utilized in this way becomes an ally in life to be looked after and cherished, rather than an adversary only to be sloughed off as some filthy thing at some later point. The body in this way becomes an investiture rather than a metaphysical burden.

95 M. Stanley-Baker, "Palpable Access to the Divine: Daoist Medieval Massage, Visualisation and Internal Sensation," *Asian Medicine* 7 (2012): 101–27.

Even still, death will come. It is best to be mindful of attachment or clinging to the bodily form so that it can be avoided. This is, after all, one of the pathways toward ghostliness.

The Embodiment

Wang Fengyi tells us in no uncertain terms that the body is a necessary component of a life lived according to the Dao. We have a Bodily Nature (xing) which ought to be refined and cultivated as one requisite step toward attainment of the Dao.

The key to this refinement and cultivation of the body, indeed its transformation from mere sheath of flesh animated by the mind and spirits into a vital component of an open and expanding destiny, is work:

> To make the Realm of the Inner Nature pure, harbor Virtue. To make the Realm of the Heart pure, illuminate the Heavenly principle inside you (mingli). *To make the Realm of the Body pure, increase your practical skills.* Virtue is able to nurture the Inner Nature, the Heavenly Principle is able to nurture the Heart, and *practical skills are able to nurture the Body*...It is only through genuine actions and genuine results that a person can be a ["true person"; zhēnrén, 真人].[96]

To embody this passage, one need only practice the skills that one knows or that one wishes to know better.

Sing or play an instrument. What sounds are coming? What are your hands or feet doing? How much pressure is necessary to work your instrument?

Practice fishing. What scents or sounds are available to you? How much turbulence is in the water? If you are on a boat or moving dock, how does your body respond to the rippling of the water?

Type at your computer. What kind of pressure is necessary to depress the button? Is it too little or too much? What sound does it make?

96 Fengyi, *Twelve Characters*, 31.

JOHN ANDERSON

176

Knit or crochet. How do the needles move? Notice the weight and texture of the material you are using. What do your materials look like? Notice the pattern emerging from the work you are doing.

Draw back and release the bow. What muscles tighten or release in the process of this?

Prepare, cook, and eat food. What smells arise? What flavors do you experience as you taste, mindfully, the food you have prepared?

Become keenly aware of your body as it performs mundane, everyday tasks. Find quiet joy and contentment in the tasks that you embody and allow yourself to experience that enjoyment. At the same time, when performing baneful, quotidian tasks that you do not enjoy, allow yourself room to become acutely aware of why you dislike them. In any activity, strive to know what role your body has in it and to be aware of that role taking place in the moment. Attend to what it means to be in your body, how it feels to be in a body. It may not always be comfortable, but it is yours and only yours.

To this point be mindful: do not overly concern yourself with the workings of other forms, or of what is the perfect "form." There is no perfect body, to the body. There is a body that we possess which invariably is undeveloped in some fashion, but imperfection of form and function is in the Mind.

Pay attention to your interiorized being, your "gut" feelings, and any anomalous exterior senses. Practice of any type performed at this level needs the body, and the body can, under the right circumstances, allow us access to the ever more subtle layers of being.[97]

Thus, in Daoism and in many forms of Buddhism, one finds that

---

97   One pertinent example of this type of practice is the act of self-massage used in Daoist practice. Take for example the technique revealed to Lady Weng:

> While lying down at night first tightly close the eyes and face east. Using [the base of] the thumbs and the rear of the palms, on both the left and right, press the eyes, wipe back towards the Gate of the Ear, and cause both palms to completely meet together behind the neck twenty-seven times. Visualise in the eyes—there ought to be three colours of qì (purple, blue-green, and red)—which emerge before the eyes. This is an internal pressing of the three pure clouds, which irrigates and harmonises the eyeball-child (童子). (Stanley-Baker, "Palpable Access to the Divine")

In modern understanding, this effect is the result of stimulating the rods and cones within the eyes. From the Daoist perspective, the simple act of pressing gently on the eyes creates a visual effect indicative of the participation of and with elements of the divine.

even when one is working to strengthen the body, one also helps to cultivate the spirit within oneself. In the animist approach to Daoism contained herein, it means that cultivating the body also cultivates the native Shén spirits within each of us. Even more so, one comes up against the reality that within Daoism, the body cannot be separated from the workings of the Shén spirits, nor is it separable from the deep experiences that we all have, and that, in addition, any idea that we in the West might have of "mind" is similarly inseparable from the function (or at least existence of) the physical body. It is the natural state of the human being for the body to be lived in and lived through, for certain kinds of experience. Presence within the body is therefore part of the overall cultivation of the individual and the narrative of the self.

To Be Humane

Allow yourself the viscerality of your experience. Not that you need necessarily to attend to your body exclusively, for there is more to be had in the world, but do not ignore or denigrate its importance to your existence.

We have been given a human form that is different from other forms or body structures, and we derive the background of our experience from this form.

It is the human form, the human body, which informs the very basis of the sense of humanity, rén (人), as an embodied virtue practice. A thing cannot be embodied without a body, a cohered scaffold upon which and through which experience arises.

In short, even if you view the body as a vessel for some deeper level of experience, revel in the form that you have for what it can do rather than shun it for what it cannot do. By the same measure, hold the bodies of others with equanimity in a way that acknowledges the position in which each body places the individual.

脆骨：

天之道和地之道是相同的，只是人類之間的作用。

橋接，完善和超越天地原理是我們的職責！

而且我們並不總是知道我們在做什麼

這是適當的。

Cuìgú:

Tiān zhīdào hé de zhī dào shì xiāngtóng de, zhǐshì rénlèi zhī jiān de zuòyòng.

Qiáojiē, wánshàn hé chāoyuè tiāndì yuánlǐ shì wǒmen de zhízé!

Érqiě wǒmen bìng bù zǒng shì zhī dào wǒmen zài zuò shénme.

Zhè shì shìdàng de.

稚子气概：

天堂不是"完美"，地球也不是"不完美"。

兩者都以自己的方式展開。

要知道這兩者都是從頭腦開始的。

頭腦始於沉神。

Zhìzǐ Qìgài:

Tiāntáng bùshì "wánměi", dìqiú yě bùshì "bù wánměi".

Liǎng zhě dōu yǐ zìjǐ de fāngshì zhǎnkāi.

Yào zhīdào zhè liǎng zhě dōu shì cóng tóunǎo kāishǐ de.

Tóunǎo shǐ yú chén shén.

脆骨：

頭腦是一回事，很多事。

…

這是五種精神相互契合的。

Tóunǎo shì yī huí shì, hěnduō shì.

…

Zhè shì wǔ zhǒng jīngshén xiānghù qìhé de.

On the Mind

"Brittle Bones":

Wherefrom does emptiness become being?

Ask yourself!

For the Way of Heaven and the Way of Earth are the same, all but for mankind's role between them.

It is our role to bridge, to refine, and to transgress the principles of Heaven and Earth!

And we don't always know what we are doing.

This is appropriate.

"Baby's Breath":

Heaven is not "perfect" and Earth is not "imperfect."

Both unfold in their Ways.

To know both of these begins with the mind.

The mind begins with the Shén spirits.

"Brittle Bones":

The Mind is one thing and many.

It is the Heart-mind consciousness, it is the Heart-mind within the Heart-mind.

It is the coming and going of the twelve officials.

It is the accordance of the Five Shén with one another.

COMMENTARY

As with many overarching philosophical frameworks, a comprehensive theory of mind is far and away one of the most difficult discussions to be had. This is no less true in the eastern philosophical traditions, and as with most philosophical traditions, this set of ideas has evolved over time. Even today, there are many theories of mind folded into the broad set of ideas expressed within the broad set of cultural traditions from the Han dynasty (~220 BCE–~206 CE) into the present.

The mind in these frameworks is not entirely localized, and is, in many respects, not entirely dependent on the brain as a locus for consciousness.[98] It consists of vast amounts of information which we are not altogether conscious of unless we are paying specific attention in a mindful manner, such as what occurs in many forms of contemplation or meditation. The mind is a constellation of information that must be taken in and "digested" or interpreted so as to make any of it useable. This web of information finds each of us as a "node" of shifting potentials and capacities which coalesces into a loose composite of psychic and sensory structures.[99]

There are several models for the psyche within the Chinese tradition, including the Nine Palace model frequently encountered in many branches of religious and esoteric Daoism. The recognition of the "Mud Ball" (i.e., the physical brain) as the seat of Being, and the Wushén or "Five Spirit" framework which is ubiquitous in popular Chinese folk traditions and carried through into the modern world within the synthesized correspondences of Chinese medicine, itself anchored by ancient, if perhaps incomplete works such as the *Huangdi Neijing Suwen (The Yellow Emperor's Inner Classic—Simple Questions)* and

---

98 The Daoist name for the brain is in fact "Mud Ball." This shows the typical Daoist turn toward deemphasis of the structure itself.

99 The concept of the "nouome" is introduced here to outline the whole of one's psyche as well as the many functions of the psyche and the many ways in which it can be influenced (environment, quality of exposure, the effect of jīng-essence of the lineage (which extends beyond the direct contribution of the parents or the grandparents. It is meant to provide a correlate structure to the concept of the "biome" as it is encountered in modern biology.

the *Huangdi Neijing Lingshu (The Yellow Emperor's Inner Classic—Spirit Pivot).*[100]

Any discussion of the Mind according to Daoist syncretism quickly becomes very complicated for most readers. In an attempt to remedy this, and to avoid undue confusion, we will confine our discussion to the Five Spirit or Wushén model, as modern sources and commentary are readily available to those who wish to explore the deeper aspects of the psyche according to Daoism and Chinese folk knowledge. Here, we will lay out each of the Wushén as separate principles (as they are commonly glossed in most modern clinical contexts), or even as separate entities (as they are approached in the present text) in order that the role of each can be better understood as the participation of a part to the greater function of the whole of the "present" psychological experience.[101]

The upshot: we are composite beings, physically as well as mentally, comprised of forms, structures, or entities which have, to a greater or lesser extent, their own needs, agency, and occasionally, their own drives, all of which are under ideal circumstances, moderated, facilitated and largely expressed by the work of the singular Shén spirit which "resides" in the heart (Xīn). Together, the other four Shén provide information to the singular Shén which works to make sense of it, filtering out material to help construct meaning for a person within a given situation.

That is to say that the singular Shén spirit housed within the physical Xīn (heart), gives rise to Xīn (Heart/Mind).

JOHN ANDERSON

100 The second of the two provides a system of psyche which is just as esoteric as any of those posited by Daoist magical doctrine and practice. There is, in the Wǔshén (Five Spirit 五神) framework of the psyche an emphasis on the cultivation and use of entities or capacities, which are somehow more innate than the spirits invoked in specific Daoist lineages. In this line of thinking, one does not need spirit registers of entities to be present. One already has access to the collective Shén by virtue of incarnation.

101 This idea does not translate easily into English. It is proposed herein that this gestalt of psychic components and the resulting mental processes amounts to a "nouome" in the same way that the totality of cellular function of the gut is referred to as a "biome."

The Five Shén

In accordance with the Five Phase system of relational correspondence that has been an essential part of Chinese philosophy and folk-practices for millennia, each of us are home to five Shén (spirits), which, when regarded as a whole are similarly called Shén, and which are spearheaded by one of the five spirits that is itself also referred to as the Shén. This is utterly confusing if one does not have pretext. For our purposes here, the Five Shén references the group of internalized entities residing in each of us, of which the singular Shén is but one exemplar. It is important to remind oneself as the text unfolds that the Wushén are the Five Spirits within the individual person *and* that these spirits are said to oversee various aspects of the Mind. Modern use of the Shén often reduces them to their epiphenomenal functions, but in their ancient form, the Wushén were seen as complete and discreet members of a whole organism charged with performing some part of being by Heaven and given form by essence.

In addition to the individualized materiality of the essences, the five solid organs (zàng) become the centralized locus for the be invisible, yet palpable world which each of us embodies:

> "[T]he five zàng are the storage of essences/spirits Jingshén, blood and breaths, xuè[102]/qì, the Hún, and the Pò.[103]

The Shén spirits are still primary, even in this case.

Let us examine each in further detail.

The Shén

The Shén is the central "spirit-of-a-being" itself. It is related to the Fire Element. It resides in the heart, is related to the frontal lobes of the brain, and is the animating spirit of our conscious awareness.

102 This vitalized form of blood will be covered in greater detail in a subsequent volume.
103 Larre and Rochat de la Vallee, *Rooted in Spirit*, 7.

One of the main roles of the singular Shén is to provide a means toward coherence to the many chaotic and so often, competing streams of qualitative consciousness, rather than more quantitative aspects represented by specific "rational" thought processes and other functions of the Mind. Knowing when to take in and when to "cross the great stream" into the world. The affirmative impulse in the face of the world.

Cosmological reference: the mountain peak above the clouds and the light of the sun, moon and stars that shine down from heaven.

The Hún

The Hún is the "Ethereal" Soul. It is related to the Wood Element. It resides in the liver and is the animating spirit of our imagination, vision and planning capacities. The Hún is different from the Shén but close to it, following closely as the Shén move between Heaven and Earth. The Hún regulates the functions of intuition, sleep, dreaming, and day-dreaming. When it is directed, the Hún looks forward into the future with clarity of vision. Able to see and interact with more than one possible future, it is always just slightly "ahead" in "time."

This is why the Hún is the coming-and-going of the Shén.

Cosmological reference: the misty cloud forests of the mountain cliffs.

The Yì

The Yì is the Intention. It is also seen as the "intellect" in some currents of Chinese folk tradition, and is therefore directly related to acts of cogitation and calculation. It is related to the Earth Element. It resides in the spleen and is the animating spirit of our muscles, and has to do with our potency, our power, our ability to burn the fuel of food and life energy so that we are able to "do" what we need to do to create our life.

Psychologically it is this Shén which allows us to plant our feet properly so we can keep moving in the manner of the ox in the fields. The Yì is steadiness and constancy. Finding the middle ground of being, this is the Realm of Humankind. Knowing your limits and acknowledging available resources.

Security, boundaries, and wholeness as physicalized processes.

Cosmological reference: the fertile fields at the horizon line between the upper mountain and the underworld.

The Pò

The Pò is the Animal Soul. It is related to the Metal Element. It resides in the lungs during life, the large intestine at birth and death, and is the animating spirit of the autonomic nervous system. It is the spirit which helps us to cut through, to discern "good" from "bad" or "pleasant" from "harmful." It is responsible for enacting the instincts and protecting the individual from the "slings and arrows of outrageous fortune."

Looking to specific events in the past, and in some cases, reliving them. Instinctual drives acted out. The Pò oversees the needs of survival, and boundaries overtaken by others. Repetitive patterns usually beyond our conscious control.

Cosmological reference: the labyrinths and caves below the sacred mountain. The "upper" underworld and the unconscious drives which are just below the surface.

The Zhì

The Zhì is the Will. It is related to the Water Element. It resides in the kidneys and is the animating spirit of our instincts and our wisdom. When the term will is invoked here, it is the first impulse toward a thing, as well as the will to power. Recognition of Ming as the organizing template of one's existence is also found here. However, perseverance toward the expression of one's destiny falls under the steadfast dependability of the Yì, mentioned above.

Cosmological reference: the sulfurous hot springs that shoot up from the darkest deepest recesses of the caverns below the mountain.[104] This is the stored heat at the center of the earth. It is from this heat that forms will eventually arise or be overtaken. There is, with this Shén, the space of destruction, continuation, and change.Deep aspects of genetic potential and old lineage. The "deep" underworld and the deep unconscious.

All of these constituent, independent parts of the psyche, alive with qì of their own, work to assure the existence and function of the Heart-mind. Through this, one lives in accordance with Heaven. One should be careful to guard the Heart-mind, which stems from the ancestral qì which each of us has inherited. Conversely, one ought not place as much of an emphasis on the intellectuality of mind.

The *Neiye* (*Inner Chapters of the Zhuangzi*)[105] offers the following on the role of the Heart mind and its downfall:

> When my heart is orderly, my senses are orderly;
> When my heart is peaceful, my senses are peaceful.
> What sets them in order is the heart-mind;
> What makes them peaceful is the heart-mind.
> The heart-mind conceals another heart-mind.
> Within the center of the heart-mind, there is another
>   heart-mind.
> In this heart of the heart-mind,
> There is a resonance (intention) which precedes words.
> Resonance is followed by forms;
> Forms are followed by words;

JOHN ANDERSON

104 Lorie Dechar "Wu Shen—The Five Spirits." https://www.anewpossibility.com/wp-content/uploads/2016/06/Wu-Shen_UK-2015.pdf [Last accessed 6 Dec 2020].

105 Dan G. Reid, *The Thread of Dao: Unraveling Early Daoist Oral Traditions in Guan Zi's Purifying the Heart-Mind (Bai Xīn), Art of the Heart-Mind (Xīn Shu), and Internal Cultivation (Nei Ye)* (Montreal: Center Ring, 2019), 238–39.

Words are followed by directives;
Directives are followed by order.[106]
When there is disorder, there is sure to be confusion.
Confusion leads to death.

This idea of Heart-mind (Xīn) still permeates contemporary clinical practice in Traditional Chinese Medicine as well as much of meditative and ritual practice, but it is not, by any means the oldest concept of mind or emotion to be had within what would become Chinese culture as it is seen today, at least by some accounts.

In the present text, the psyche is seen as being the cooperation between the Five Shén as semi-autonomous entities which each have their own interrelated capacities and realities as well as greater or lesser states of agency, which in turn contribute to the conscious experience of the person who houses them. This also means that there may be times when the Shén begin to act of their own accord in a manner which is deleterious to the person. This is most often the outcome of trauma or neglect which serves to harm or malnourish one or more of the Shén.

The Embodiment

Zhuangzi states:

> Nothing is more Shén than Heaven.
> Heaven and Earth are perfectly Shén.
> The way to preserve the Shén is to preserve one's jīng in unadulterated purity. It is by his Jing-Shén that the sage mirrors the myriad things in the stillness of his heart.[107]

---

106 Given the structure of this passage, it seems as if there is a missing sentence here. In this logic, the next sentence would say something to the effect of "Order is followed by disorder."

107 Harold D. Roth, *A Companion to Angus Graham's Chuang Tzu* (Honolulu: University of Hawai'i Press, 2003).

In the *Lingshu*, we are given a stance from which to approach the preservation of Shén:

> The wise nourish life by flowing with the four seasons and adapting to cold or heat, by harmonizing joy and anger in a tranquil dwelling, by balancing yin and yang, and what is hard and soft. So it is that dissolute evil cannot reach the man of wisdom, and he will be witness to a long life.[108]

To be in alignment with this:

Eat well, but only what you need, and in accordance with the seasons and your own constitution.

Rest well, but only what you need, and in accordance with the seasons and your own constitution.

Hone your senses and your skills. Know when to pull away from both.

Find tranquility and work toward equanimity. This is the balancing of Yin and Yang. In this way, your Wushén will settle and clear as mud settles in still water.

Do not live solely in your head, lest your own directives give rise to disorder. Do not let the Mud Ball cloud the clarity of the Shén as they go about their movement and work.

Let yourself live in your body. The embodiment spoken to in this passage is one which cannot be intellectualized, although it may begin with this level of knowledge. It must be a felt process.

To be clear, there is no one specific exercise which will put one in touch with the Shén. Your spirits are your own, and they must be ex-

108 Larre and Rochat de la Valle, *Rooted in Spirit*, 64.

cavated in whatever fashion is available to you. They are autonomous in their own right, but they are still you.

The onus lies upon each of us to go digging in our bones to find the spirits, and further to treat them with the respect that companions and colleagues and co-creators deserve.

In some cases they only need to be reminded of their place and roles, in others, they must be revived by proper care, feeding, and encouragement, while in still other cases, the Shén may need to be exhumed, recovered, and "brought back to life." The work is different for each of us who would work to return to the Human Path.

To Be Humane

Recognize the larger work of the Shén as they issue from the mandate of Heaven, even as each is incarnated though unique and singular essences. Utilize this rare set of capacities that comprise this unique being that is you. Safeguard them and do not waste them!

They will only incarnate as you once...

稚子气概：

考慮山的形式限制山的存在！

在山頂上看山！

Zhìzǐ Qìgài:

Kǎolǜ shān de xíngshì xiànzhì shān de cúnzài!

Zài shāndǐng shàng kàn shān!

脆骨：

學會坐下。

...

如果這樣做，"您"將不再坐下。

但是坐著還是可以的！

Cuìgú:

Xuéhuì zuò xià.

...

Rúguǒ zhèyàng zuò,"nín" jiāng bù zài zuò xià.

Dànshì zuòzhe háishì kěyǐ de!

稚子气概：

在這裡，一個人真正地受束縛，並以此來移動宇宙。

Zhìzǐ Qìgài:

Zài zhèlǐ, yīgèrén zhēnzhèng de shòu shùfù, bìng yǐ cǐ lái yídòng yǔzhòu.

脆骨：

行動與不行動都需要適當的時機。

這就是"穿越大河"。

知道何時參加河水和與河一起移動是正確的。

知道什麼時候該留在銀行是正確的。

都沒錯，都是必要的。

Cuìgú:

Xíngdòng yǔ bù xíngdòng dōu xūyào shìdàng de shíjī.

Zhè jiùshì "chuānyuè dàhé".

Zhīdào héshí cānjiā héshuǐ hé yǔ hé yīqǐ yídòng shì zhèngquè de.

Zhīdào shénme shíhòu gāi liú zài yínháng shì zhèngquè de.

Dōu méicuò, dōu shì bìyào de.

On Action and Inaction

"Baby's Breath":

Contemplate the being of the mountain bound by the form of the mountain!

Contemplate the mountain on top of the mountain!

Contemplate the 54th hexagram!

What does it mean to be Bound?

"Brittle Bones":

Learn to sit down.

Learn to sit to the point of boredom.

Learn to sit past the point of boredom.

Learn to sit then to the point of contentment.

Learn to sit past the point of contentment.

If you do this, you will find discomfort.

Learn to sit past the point of discomfort.

If you do this, "you" will no longer be sitting.

But sitting is being done nonetheless!

"Baby's Breath":

It is here where one truly becomes bound, and doing this, moves the universe.

Stillness becomes the unmoving axis.

Around this is openness of exertion.

And though movement occurs,

There is no effort to it.

This is the Way!

"Brittle Bones":

Exertion is effort directed in its proper course.

Allow your effort to become effortless.

This is the turning of the cart-wheel.

This is wuwei.

But also know when rest is necessary and allow it, for it is the un-moving axle.

Without the axle the wheel does not move from a central place, can quickly become unstable.

Both action and inaction require proper timing.

This is "Crossing the Great River."

Know when it is right to wade in and move with the River.

Know when it is right to stay still on the bank.

Neither are wrong, both are necessary.

COMMENTARY

The mountain is an apt image for this passage, not only for the stillness that it represents, but also for the incipient movement, change, and growth which naturally arise from deep within the heart of this stillness.

> Sacred mountains in the Asian tradition are also stages for spirits and gods, but these denizens are somewhat gentler than the likes of Zeus and Yahweh. Rather than places where supreme deities demonstrate their awe-some power, mountains in the Asian tradition are where heavenly wisdom is received and higher spiritual states are attained, whether this is moksha, nirvana, or another form of worldly transcendence.[109]

There is a point at which we must begin to know when to act and when to let things happen. In many modern cultures, the ability to recognize when inaction is necessary is at best contemptuously tolerated, and at worst, scoffed at as a sign of nothing more than a quitter's conscience. The acceptance of inaction in modernized cultures holds even less esteem. In truth, it is often a form of moral turpitude, more akin to conscious resignation than inner cultivation.

These impressions are difficult to circumvent in many contexts. Deadlines and familial responsibilities often carry the day and allow precious little room for perceived existential lassitude. It is essential to allows stillness to take hold within our lives. It is the ability to discern the proper timing for action and in-action to take place, which allows us to maintain the balance of being necessary within a lived life. In this passage, we find represented the idea that non-action can be a useful tool. Even in the depths of inaction, however, nascent action takes place.

The key to seeing this is to sit.

JOHN ANDERSON

109 Thomas Michael, "Mountains and Early Daoism in the Writings of Ge Hong," *History of Religions* 56.1 (2016): 23–54.

The Embodiment

Learn to sit.

This is an activity that most of us do constantly, and yet we are completely ignorant of it.

There are two simple ideas which must be acknowledged when approaching the art of inaction for the types of cultivation valued within Daoism, Buddhism, and Confucianism, as these two ideas form the first conditions of cultivation within each of these applied philosophical traditions.

First, there is the establishment of the base. When one chooses to sit as part of a cultivation practice, it is incumbent on the person to have a base that is firm, broad, and steady.

Next, there is the establishment of form through ease and open-ness. In the present context, we are less concerned with rigid ideas of having the posture just so, with the breath conducted in a very spe-cific manner. Rather, we are concerned with the ease and naturalness with which one holds a given posture.[110]

To begin, establish a clear enough physical space so that distrac-tion is minimized. If possible, the space should be as insulated from external "noise" and distraction as possible.[111] The space need not be sterile, but for most, a relatively clean space is more amenable to con-sistent practice of any sort than one that is dirty. See the preceding passage "On Choosing Your Environment" for greater context in this regard.

Next there is the embrace of ease and openness in one's practice. In easiness, there is still practice that is consistent and rigorous, but which values softness or pliability over hardness and rigidity. The

110 To be clear, there are a great many forms of inner cultivation from a great many traditions that have very specific, very complex methodologies, with particular end-goals that serve to guide the practice. This passage is much concerned more with an approach sitting which is accessible and repeatable for anyone who chooses to practice it.

111 This "noise" includes modern "time sinks," such as television, phone, or internet. While each of these are tool in themselves, there is often a pull to these activities which severely undercuts the regularity, and thus, often the use of any form of internal cultivation. Music may be of use to cultivation practice if it either primes the mind or the body for the exercise at hand, or serves to negate some other noise within the practice environment.

practice should proceed from a state of equanimity such that one does not immediately become married to one form. Likewise, the ability to accept what comes allows openness to emerge.

Openness is the feeling of "flow" or movement which occurs within the body even in moments of utter tranquility and immobility.

These capacities both arise from effort and practice in the beginning, but if both ease and openness are available to one, then so too will be the ken of action, knowing when to act. In this way, action proceeds from inaction.

To Be Humane

There is a steadiness that comes from rest, and there is dynamic change which comes from action. This steadiness is only available to us when we are able to stop, to reverse or return, and from there proceed once again. To experience change is to experience the underlying constant of reality, and even if we share nothing else with anyone else, we all have this.

稚子气概：

吃飯時，要吃飽，但不要再吃了。

胃口滿意嗎？

Zhìzǐ Qìgài:

Chīfàn shí, yào chī bǎo, dàn bùyào zài chīle.

Wèikǒu mǎnyì ma?

脆骨：

當您餓了時，就餓了，但再也沒有了，

自願採取飢餓絕非一種懲罰。

Cuìgú:

Dāng nín èle shí, jiù èle, dàn zài yě méiyǒule,

zìyuàn cǎiqǔ jī'è jué fēi yīzhǒng chéngfá.

稚子气概：

確實要清楚！

您想要滋養什麼？

...

因為"青古"將像您親愛的孩子一樣輕鬆地帶走
您的食物和時間。

Zhìzǐ Qìgài:

Quèshí yào qīngchǔ!

Nín xiǎng yào zīyǎng shénme?

...

Yīnwèi "Qīnggǔ" jiāng xiàng nín qīn'ài de háizi yīyàng qīngsōng dì dài zǒu nín de shíwù hé shíjiān.

On Nourishment

"Baby's Breath":

When you eat, eat enough, but no more.

What does a sated appetite feel like?

Does the body know, itself, when it is done?

This, too, rests with awareness.

"Brittle Bones":

When you starve, starve enough, but no more,

When undertaken voluntarily, hunger is not a punishment.

Learn the art of the fast!

In this way, even when the stomach is empty, the belly remains easy and full.

"Baby's Breath":

Be clear, indeed!

For what is it you seek to nourish?

This is the counsel of the Yijing.

In providing nourishment, know what you would be feeding.

Nourish in accordance with the Xīn.

For "Old Blue" will take your food and your time just as easily as your dear children will.

COMMENTARY

The deeper ideas of nourishment (as opposed to "eating," "consuming," or "feeding") are part of the structure of most societies whose roots are deeply planted in history. The broad strokes of culture presented here are no different. We may even take the process for granted as a natural outcome of living, but there are many who, despite being animated and living, are neither vibrant nor thriving.

As a general act meant to promote and maintain the essential effulgence of and transition of being, nourishment can take on many forms. We can easily grasp the sustenance that comes with food and drink. Very often, though, there are forms of enrichment which lie outside of physical consumption. Indeed, we can see nourishment as encompassing practices or events which cannot be readily quantified, except through direct experience. Here, a woman goes to exercise, and there, a man reads a book while taking a bath. One person regards a painting and is put at peace, while another sings a hymn to a dying friend. Thus, the idea of nourishing, of nurturing, oneself or others can take place anywhere and at any time.

What is the fundamental difference between consumption and nourishment?

Consumption is a goal in itself, while nourishment is but a movement into being.

The goal of a lived life is experience, and whether one knows it or not, acts which nourish deeply are those in which we are deeply engaged, so that our boundaries fall away to nothingness. They are acts which promote a coherence of a composite-being in the moment. The Shén spirits like this.

In the opening lines to this passage, there is something of an admonishment, if not an overt warning, which cautions us to "know what it is that you are nourishing." To do this, it helps to ask, do you work to nourish your gu□ or your Shén?

Sometimes the biggest trick lies in discerning one from the other.

The "Three Corpse Worms," or Sānshīchóng (三尸蟲)

According to Daoist body cosmology, the Sānshīchóng, or more simply the Sānshī or Sānchóng, ("Three Corpses" or "Three Worms," respectively), are a triad of native indwelling spirits who have one "duty" and two overriding goals. It is the job of the Three Corpses to report the infractions of the person to the bureaucrats of Heaven. The main consequence for "bad" behavior is that allotted time is subtracted from the "host." That is, the destiny of the of the individual is foreshortened. In this sense, the Three Worms act as messengers who leave the body twice each month to even the tally of one's life.

There is one very telling problem: the "Three Corpses" are not altogether benevolent in character or aim. They, in fact, wish to feast upon the organs of individuals who are acting hosts.[112] This is readily accomplished once the host dies prematurely (i.e., once their Ming has expired). They are resilient and cunning in this calling, too, as their main mode of action is to encourage the very behaviors they will subsequently and gladly report to the recordkeepers of Heaven.

The first of the trio we encountered in the opening section of this passage. Qīnggǔ, (青古) or "Old Blue" lives in the brain, or Upper Dantian, and of this charming being, Maspero writes:

> It is he who makes men blind, or deaf, or bald, who makes the teeth fall out, who stops up the nose and gives bad breath.[113]

Wilmont adopts the more common moniker of Pengju (彭侸), or "Trinket Maker" who causes the individual to crave lavish, superfluous things.[114]

Next, we encounter Báigū (白姑) or "White Maiden," of which Maspero relays that:

JOHN ANDERSON

112 Henri Maspero, *Taoism and Chinese Religion*, tr. by Frank A. Kierman Jr., (Amherst: University of Massachusetts Press, 1981), 332.
113 *Ibid.*
114 Dennis Wilmont, *The Five Phases of Acupuncture in the Classical Texts* (Marshfield: Willmountain Press, 2009), 284.

She causes palpitations of the heart, asthma, and melancholy.[115]

Péngzhì (彭質; "Value Maker"), is the more common moniker for this unruly resident. It resides in the middle Dantian. If Pengzhi holds sway, the person will crave sensory pleasure. Beautiful sights and sounds, and scrumptious tastes and smells are the playground for the "Value Maker" as it teaches the host to prize one thing over another.[116] Péngzhì will cause one to wonder "Where is the stimulation I crave?" and will encourage its pursuit to the point of physical and mental exhaustion. Over time, this may serve to compromise the integrity of one's boundaries as the Center weakens.

Lastly, we find Xuèshī (血尸) whose name translates to "Bloody Corpse" of which is said:

> It is through him that the intestines are painfully twisted, that the bones are dried out, that the skin withers, that the limbs have rheumatisms...[117]

Also called Pengjiao (彭矯), or "Bridgemaker," it aims to have each person squander his or her effort and potential (i.e., qì and jīng), most often through sexual congress with others. It lives in the Lower Dantian, the Stomach, intestines, and genitals. The loss of essence and qì can cause muscles to weaken, motivation to wane, thus bringing one to a rut-like stillness, which, if left unchecked, can forestall the future.[118]

For most of us, what occurs during our lifetime only serves to feed the Three Corpses, and one must rid oneself of the Sānshī if one is to live out one's full allotment of days in health and happiness. This is more important still if one wishes to undertake any cultivation of numinous energies so as to increase one's lifespan or to gain præternatural abilities.

---

115 Maspero, *Taoism and Chinese Religion*, 332.
116 Willmont, *The Five Phases of Acupuncture*, 284.
117 Maspero, *Taoism and Chinese Religion*, 332.
118 Wilmont, *The Five Phases of Acupuncture*, 284.

Within the Daoist canon wherein these pernicious spirits are most commonly found, there are generally two approaches to be taken in order that one should be free of these parasites—poison or abnegation.[119] The first, that of "poison," is not advised accept under very specific conditions. It will therefore not be covered in this text as a viable method.

The second major approach to dealing with the Three Corpse Worms is that of abstention. Here, it is not necessarily strict regimens of fasting, although it can be. More commonly, it is abstention from the substances which are widely held to provide the foundation for organized society as we currently know it—the "five grains,"[120] cereal crops domesticated in order to feed a population which was becoming localized and concentrated into settlements.

The "Verse of Great Existence" (*Dayou zhang*) warns the reader about the inherent danger of grains:

> The five grains are chisels cutting life away,
> Making the five organs stink and shorten our spans.
> Once entered into our stomach,
> There's no more chance to live quite long.
> To strive for complete avoidance of all death
> Keep your intestines free of excrement![121]

---

119 In the first case one chooses to ingest materials which will be toxic to the worms, often clearing their influences and ejecting any physical traces in an abrupt and often messy manner. Such is the case with many traditional substances use to promote emesis and/or defecation such as Binglang (檳榔; areca) and Shijunzi (使君子; quisqualis) respectively. Poison substances can also be used to change the internal environment so that the Sānshī must evacuate on their own. This is the reasoning behind the use of Xionghuang (雄黃; realgar), Zhusha (辰砂; cinnabar), or Ganqi (干漆; lacquertree sap). These are all used to infuse the body with a fierce Yang qì with the Sānshī cannot easily tolerate, and in the case of Ganqi, can also coat the insides, making it impossible for the Three Corpse Worms to maintain their foothold within the body. Unfortunately, these substances are also quite deadly to the host if they are taken for extended periods or in large quantities.

120 Wǔ Gǔ (五穀)—the "Five Grains" mark the beginnings of agriculture in the Chinese tradition. There is some contention as to which five grains constitute the pentad, but one commonly finds listed: wheat, rice, foxtail millet, soy, and hemp. Other lists replace some of these with sorghum, broomcorn millet, or sesame.

121 Livia Kohn, (ed.), *The Taoist Experience: An Anthology* (Albany: SUNY Press: Albany, 1993), 150.

JOHN ANDERSON

It behooves each of us to know what we are taking in for ourselves and to know who and what we are growing within each of us. If you do not shore up the qì, the blood will be weakened, and if the blood is weakened the Shén cannot travel. If the Shén cannot move, the Jīng[122] will have no expression. When we nourish ourselves, the spirits and essences are held and nourished at the same time. When these are fed and maintained, life unfolds smoothly.

The Yijing provides the final meditation in stating:

The jūnzǐ [cultivated person] uses considerate words to inform [others],
And articulation in drinking and taking-in.[123]

Proper maintenance of the body and the Shén spirits requires discretion and discernment. Timing, quality, and preparation of anything determines how we will be nurtured by what we take in. There is no getting around this.

A Note on the Five Flavors (wǔwèi; 五味)

One of the most common conventions of nutrition found within the majority of Asian cultures is the concept of "flavors." The five flavors constitute a schema by which the action of the qualities of food and drink are matched to the body, in a circumscribed set of correspondences which most often dovetail with the five-phase system of cosmological classification.

The five flavors, or wǔ wèi; 五味 are: sweet 甜, sour 酸, bitter 苦, spicy hot 辣, salty 鹹|咸. These terms do not exactly correspond to the idea of taste which we have in the West. Rather, these terms are seen

---

122 Here, Jīng is the specific form of imbued essence which becomes the delineated "form" of the native Shén spirits within us.

123 Rudolf Ritsema and Shantena Augusto Sabbadini, *The Original I Ching Oracle or The Book of Changes* (London: Watkins, 2018), 320; This line implies a discretion or discernment in consumption, both in "active" consumption, as when one "chews through" something to get at the center of it, as the name of this hexagram "The Jaws" implies, as well as in more "passive" consumption, such as when fluid flows down the throat unobstructed. Both require a mindful, discerning approach.

as a form of shorthand for the qualities of the substance and its over-all impact on the body (and mind). They have the following function-al tendencies and affinities within the body:

- Sweet corresponds to the Earth phase. In modern usage, the organ most often associated with it is the spleen.
- Functionally, the sweet flavor tends to build muscles and flesh.
- Sour corresponds to the Wood phase. In modern usage, the organ most often associated with it is the liver.
- Functionally the sour flavor tends to contract and pull inward.
- Bitter corresponds to the Fire phase. In modern usage, the organ most often associated with it is the heart.
- Functionally, the better flavor serves to disperse and clear the internal milieu of the body.[124]
- Spicy/pungent corresponds to the Metal phase. In modern usage, the organ most often associated with it is the lung.
- Functionally, the spicy/pungent flavor tends to open, disperse, and clear the external milieu.[125]
- Salty corresponds to the Water phase. In modern usage, the organ most often associated with the salty flavor is the kidney.
- Functionally, salty tends to dissolve internal accumulations.

From this short explanation, two points must be made. First, in this schema, the "nutritional" value of food and drink is secondary to the qì of the food as a whole, that is, the totality of its qualities, its qì, directly affects the qì of the individual. Second, even though specific organs are listed as points of contact for food and drink and the quali-

124 In this case, the change in the nutritive environment allows the body to properly address pathogens that have settled into the layers of the body, or other conditions which affect the deeper internal function of the body as a whole.

125 In simple terms, it does this by mobilizing and clearing the defensive qì of the individual. This outermost layer of qì serves to protect the individual from invasive sources.

ties which they possess, it must be stressed that the qì of one's food and drink affects the body in totality, the mind in totality, and the spirit in totality.[126]

In addition to knowing the proper qì of food and drink, it is also useful to remember the following:

Know when it is proper to ingest and when one is satiated. Be mindful of the constant want to consume, if it should arise.

Consume quality. Know where your nourishment comes from.

As you take anything in, be it physical sustenance or otherwise, be mindful of how it is prepared and presented, with the caveat that beautiful presentation does not imply proper preparation.

All of this is vital because it all pertains to the Shén through the building of essence:

> When you assimilate various kinds of foods, you build...your essences, and from these essences, you will be able to manifest the spirits [Shén] which are working within you. The spirits from heaven are your own, but they are only your own because of the specific pattern which is given by the essences [jīng]."[127]

Be mindful of what you are nourishing. It is more desireable to nourish the Jingshén than the Sānshī, even if both forms of spirit are found within us.

The Embodiment

The ways in which one can embody this passage are limitless, with the following in mind: to nourish, one must go into the process with awareness.

126 The move toward reducing the function of the flavor to one organ specifically is a reductionist one and one which, in many ways, stands in stark contrast to the themes of wholeness and coherence which each of us drives to embody even as we are composed of different layers of being, and beings. The esoteric effect of the flavors as qì on the Shén spirits will be addressed more completely in a subsequent volume.

127 Larre and Rochat de la Vallee, *The Heart in Lingshu*, 16. Note: Jīng is the material expression to which the Shén spirits connect. A future passage presents the motif of the spirits being attached to, or perhaps attuned with, the Blood. It is the jīng component of the Blood that allows this connection. Jīng, in this regard is instantiated vitality.

What am I eating?

What does it taste like? What flavors can I discern?

What texture does it have?

More generally, we are also nourished by what we choose to do for ourselves.

Does this action or engagement allow me to move in a less constricted manner or does it prevent eventualities in an undue fashion?

Another means by which to understand the embodiment of this passage: begin by observing how you react when you skip a meal, or can't have a certain kind of meal.

How does your body feel?

How do you react emotionally if you miss a meal?

Which of your Shén do you think are being affected, and why?

The goal in this case is to support the needs of the individual in all aspects of life, and diet is paramount. This has been recognized in Chinese culture for millennia, but even modern media is beginning to catch wind of this.[128]

The state of the qì and the blood are the origin and matrix of life and of experience and hence are of the greatest import here. In the Chinese folk custom, and in Chinese popular culture alike, food and drink can be used directly to build and sustain many aspects of the being. Even the most subtle expressions of being are subject to this. This view also emphasizes that food and drink can also be harmful, as certain foods can change the digestive processes, often by introducing "heat" or "cold" into the system or by creating unwanted byproducts, such as the aforementioned "phlegm."

Let us examine foods used to fortify two substances in particular, the qì and the blood as the "post-heaven" prima materia.

Foods to Strengthen Qì

Foods especially useful to tonify Qì Deficiency through the Earth Phase:

JOHN ANDERSON

128 Elizabeth Berenstein, "The Food That Helps Battle Depression," *The Wall Street Journal* (2 April 2018): https://www.wsj.com/articles/the-food-that-helps-battle-depression-1522678367 [Last accessed 25 June 2019].

- Grains: oats, rice, sweet rice
- Vegetables: potato, squash, sweet potato, yam
- Fruit: cherries, dates, figs, grapes, longan
- Bean product: tofu
- Meat: beef, chicken, goose, ham, lamb
- Herbs: licorice (gancao)
- Oils/condiments: molasses

Foods to Build the Blood

- Grains: barley, corn, oats, rice, sweet rice, wheat, bran
- Vegetables: alfalfa sprout, artichoke, beetroot, button mushroom, cabbage, celery, dandelion leaf, dark leafy greens, kelp, shiitake mushroom, spinach, watercress, wheatgrass
- Fruit: apple, apricot, avocado, date, fig, grape, longan, mulberry
- Beans: aduki, black soya, kidney
- Nuts and seeds: almonds, black sesame
- Fish: mussel, octopus, oyster, sardine, tuna
- Meat: all red meat especially bone marrow and liver (beef, pork, sheep)
- Dairy: chicken egg,
- Herbs, spices: nettle, parsley
- Oils, condiments: amasake, molasses
- Beverages: soy milk

The general recommendation here: fresh meats and vegetables. Clean food is preferable to heavily processed foods. It is this freshness which assures the vitality of the food, even when cooked. Other dietary guidelines include:

Seasonal eating: Eating according to the seasons is very important as our bodies also go through cyclical shifts. It is crucial to understand that we are taking in the qì of the food and drink that we consume, and it is valuable to understand that foods entertain different qualities throughout the year. One would not generally want cold foods in the cooler months, as these can tend to snuff out the fire of the digestion. Very hot foods may also damage the digestion if taken during the warmer months.

Regional eating: Being aware of the foods which naturally occur in a region or which are native to it can be vital, particularly if there is a strong bio-regional connection between an individual and a region. Indeed, to further observe the effect that material nourishment can have on the qì of an individual, one need only realize how quickly homesickness might be assuaged with just a few bites of a regional dish well prepared.

Eating at regular intervals and being mindful of the timing of meals (organ clock): The Earth Phase, which is responsible for digestion loves a routine, so eating at regular times of the day can help keep the body at its optimal state.

Eat well, but in moderate amounts. Listen carefully to the body, here. Recognize the feeling of fullness or of satisfaction.[129] The Earth Phase (i.e., the Spleen and Stomach) have difficulty effectively digesting food and distributing the essences of the food (gǔqì; 穀氣) when one has overeaten. Likewise, not eating enough may leave the body, qì, and blood malnourished or dehydrated leading to complications such as constipation, decreased immune response, or delays in wound healing.

Be wary of the overconsumption of cold or raw foods. These can slow down our physiological processes and douse our digestive fires.[130] As a modern convention, Chinese dietary guidelines gener-

129 This recognition can be difficult for some for a wide array of reasons. Do not be overly critical here. For many of us, food and drink are socially sanctioned means of "feeling good." Sit with your choices and listen to what the body feels. Work with this as a starting point.

130 The Middle Jiao, the central energetic division of the body, is commonly represented as a cooking pot. The heat provided by the Yang of the Lower Jiao should be relatively low and slow, but sustained. This will serve to create the vaporous forms of qì, which is to be distributed throughout the body without burning the contents of the Stomach.

ally advise one to stay away from cold or raw substances like ice water, smoothies, or salads in large amounts and for extended periods *unless* the seasonal conditions are very warm *and* the Yang of the individual is robust. Ideally, according to this framework, food should be at least lightly cooked (e.g., steamed), and fluids, if they are taken with the meal, should be room temperature, or above.

As with all else, be attentive to the body's response.

Foods which engender heaviness, or which are sweet, fatty or oily should be taken only in small amounts, as these will create "damp" or "phlegmatic" states in the body which will affect the movement and distribution of qì throughout the body.

Cook and eat mindfully: Take time to cook and eat. Slow down. Minimize distractions and stressors whenever possible and chew your food thoroughly.

Enjoy the experience as best you can.[131]

After you have eaten, rest for a few minutes by sitting calmly. After this, find time to engage in gentle exercise so as to help bolster the digestive function.

Stir your inner pot slowly.

Nourishment Through Herbal Praxis

A wonderfully mild formula which emulates and encourages this: Ganmai Dazao Tang. This is one of the gentlest formulas found in the Chinese pharmacopeia, and one whose simplicity allows it to be used easily and over long periods of time; something which also points to the way in which nourishment is used in this passage.

As a formula, Ganmai Dazao Tang works to bolster one's energy and to enrich the blood. It therefore has a calming effect on the Shén spirits. As with the other formulæ outlined above, the functions of the individual ingredients can point to insight as to the manner in which we can nurture ourselves in a broader sense, as well as the more immediate effect of the herbal formula itself.

---

131 For some, food and drink are complicated or even fraught subjects. If change is desired, and is to take place, this mindful, attentive approach can serve to provide the first seeds of change through awareness.

Ganmai Dazao Tang

Fúxiǎomài (*Semen Tritici*; 浮小麦)
Dàzǎo (*Fructus Jujube*; 大枣)
Zhìgāncǎo (*Radix Glycerrhizæ* 炙甘草)

Fúxiǎomài , or "wheat berry' works to tonify or strengthen the qì of the body as a whole. More specifically, this is accomplished by shoring up the function of the digestion (i.e., the Middle Jiao), as this is the material base from which the qì is formed.

Dàzǎo, or "Chinese date" serves in a secondary role to support the Fu xiao mai in tonifying qì and is also useful for providing support to the blood in its physiological and psychic functions as they are found in Chinese medicine and folk custom alike.

Zhìgāncǎo, or "prepared licorice root" plays the form that it so often plays within a vast number of herbal formulas, namely, that it mediates and modulates the other ingredients within the formula. In addition, the prepared gāncǎoalso has an effect on both the qì and Blood, and further has an affinity for the Heart. This formula therefore also helps to reseat the Shén.

In this formula, we encounter the basic truth that, for us to be fully installed in the world, we must fortify many different parts of ourselves at once. Whether it addresses the gross components such as the flesh, or the subtleties of the spirit, this is the nourishment we all need to proceed in life.

Other Forms of Nourishment

This idea of choosing one's nourishment also extends to other forms of consumption and intake. This can include how we choose to interact with others in the world, both the seen and unseen.

Here, one should choose one's companions carefully whenever possible. If transformation is one of the goals of a human life, it benefits each to foster and maintain relations with those who will help one change in an open manner. In return, one can provide some of the soil for the same ground of mutation.

While earlier passages focused on the importance of keeping your own central emptiness within the world and amongst others as a foundational stance, here, one is encouraged to be nourished by others in order to affect change in being; both are necessary, both are complementary.

Be mindful of the influence that others have on you and the influence that you might have on others. Just as with the food and drink above, ask yourself what and how you are feeling when around other people. Are you inspired or emptied, inured or awed by your company, and how are they responding to your presence?

Do not be afraid to question the actions or assumptions of others, or of yourself.

What am I doing for my experience by engaging in a behavior? Does it contribute to openness and change, ease and freedom?

Even if this examination is wholly internalized, it may still be useful.

Give to others without reciprocity when it is appropriate and when you are energized by it. Remember that we interact with others at the level of the Shén first. The qì of people will meet before physical contact is made.

Do not be afraid to share with others!

Any "food for thought" should similarly be of high quality whenever possible. That is, the information we indulge in and consume is vital to our capacity for change. Know the workings of the information that you consume.

By the same token, this means that we may need to hold our social institutions to the same standards as we do our friends. That is, if teachings or practices do not add to our experience, they deserve to be reevaluated, and, if found deeply wanting, abandoned or rebuilt. The onus of this critical examination lies with the individual, as institutions rarely are able to turn this gaze upon themselves with the same rigor or focused determination.

A Note on Abstention

At the opening to this passage, one was cautioned to know what one was feeding. the Sānshīchóng (三尸蟲), or "Three Corpse Worms" are part of Daoist body cosmology which put the importance of this in stark relief.

Change of diet has been one of the main ways to rid oneself of the Three Worms, through abstention from grains and, in some traditions, sugar and meat. This practice, known as bìgǔ (辟穀) invites one to change the internal environment of the body, and subsequently the Heart-mind.[132] In the long tradition of Chinese dietetics this is most often due to the ability of grains and sugars to engender "phlegm" which is said to weigh down the body and cloud the mind. Physiologically, we can understand this heaviness of body and obscuring of the senses[133] as being a byproduct of inflammation, which can also wreak havoc on the mind, and it is this which prevents the Shén spirits[134] from emerging fully into the world.

It should be emphasized that this particular practice is not necessarily a universal fast, although a total fast may be undertaken as a component of more advanced bìgǔ practice. In broader practice, the person would choose a limited diet of nutrient dense foods which would help to modify the internal environment of the body and to sate hunger enough to allow for the practitioner to engage in meditation, visualization, daoyin, or other exercise during the period of abstention.[135]

Bìgǔ is an involved practice and should not be undertaken lightly.[136] The same can be said of other fasting practices. The act of nega-

132 This type of practice is seen as a prerequisite to spiritual attainment in a great many traditions. As a general rule, these should not be engaged without the guidance of an appropriate medical professional.

133 Think of the ways in which the senses of taste or smell or even hearing can be affected when we are ill and our body begins to produce an overabundance of mucus.

134 The Pò and the Shen in particular are susceptible to this occultation of perception.

135 The foods used in this context varied greatly by time and region, but included ingredients such as: pine resin, sesame, pepper, ginger, and calamus, walnuts, goji berries, asparagus, Solomon's seal, atractylodes, lingzhi mushrooms, and even fushui ("talisman water").

136 See Catherine Despeux, "Bigu 辟穀 abstention from cereals," in Fabrizio Pregadio, (ed.), *The Encyclopedia of Taoism* (London: Routledge, 2008), 233-34, and Shawn Arthur, "Life Without Grains: Bigu and The Daoist Body," in Livia Kohn, *Daoist Body Cultivation:*

JOHN ANDERSON

218

tion can be uncomfortable for a variety of reasons, but there are times when the ability to gain distance from a thing is the most nurturing thing we can do. There are times when absence can begin to rebuild and refill.

Do not be afraid if this is what must be done.

To Be Humane

It is vital that we receive that which is germane to us, which sustains us, which nourishes us, and which fulfills us. This is a must and a bare minimum at that. It is hard to work toward the needs of others when our own needs are left unfulfilled. It is extremely difficult to help others achieve openness, movement, and freedom when we ourselves are starved to the point of weakness on any level, whether this is physiological, psychological, or spiritual, and it is why this most ordinary piece of human existence is so necessary, yet so often overlooked.

> *Sustain others!*
> *Feed yourself!*
> *Let others feed you!*
> *But know what you feed.*
> *Thusly do we give the Heart what it needs,*
> *Giving sustenance to our altars of being, the Yì and the Zhì.*
> *We calm our own ghosts,*
> *And exalt our spirits and our souls,*
> *Through building our Essences.*
> *This is the Way of the Vermillion Spirit.*

Traditional Models And Contemporary Practices (Honolulu: University of Hawaii Press, 2006) for a greater treatment of the subject within the historical context.

稚子气概：

三匈奴高高在上，七個便士被卡在身體上。

個人的魄與這七個較小的"靈魂"有關，並且經常將其徵召入伍。

也就是說，七個魄是行動中的魄（魄力）。

七個魄是形式上的魄.

Zhìzǐ Qìgài:

Sān xiōngnú gāogāozàishàng, qī gè biànshì bèi kǎ zài shēntǐ shàng.

Gèrén de Pò yǔ zhè qī gè jiào xiǎo de "línghún" yǒuguān, bìngqiě jīngcháng jiāng qí zhēngzhào rùwǔ.

Yě jiùshì shuō, qī gè pò shì xíngdòng zhōng de Pò (pòlì).

Qī gè pò shì xíngshì shàng de Pò.

脆骨：

毒藥到底怎麼了？

神農聖人必須品嚐所有植物，才能知道其中的哪些植物可以用來治愈。 這也意味著他有毒植物。

有時候，毒藥是治療方法。

Cuìgú:

Dúyào dàodǐ zěnmeliǎo?

Shénnóng shèngrén bìxū pǐncháng suǒyǒu zhíwù, cáinéng zhīdào qízhōng de nǎxiē zhíwù kěyǐ yòng lái zhìyù. Zhè yě yìwèizhe tā yǒudú zhíwù.

Yǒu shíhòu, dúyào shì zhìliáo fāngfǎ.

稚子气概：

我們每個人都生活在一個充滿了情感，有時甚至被情感熏陶的世界中。

它們既是人類又是活死人鬼的煉金術的一部分。

有一件重要的事情要知道：即使是幽靈也可以被引導到不同的思維和感覺方式。

Zhìzǐ Qìgài:

Wǒmen měi gèrén dōu shēnghuó zài yīgè chōngmǎnle qínggǎn, yǒu shí shènzhì bèi qínggǎn xūntáo de shìjiè zhōng.

Tāmen jìshì rénlèi yòu shì huó sǐrén guǐ de liànjīn shù de yībùfèn.

Yǒuyī jiàn zhòngyào de shìqíng yào zhīdào: Jíshǐ shì yōulíng yě kěyǐ bèi yǐndǎo dào bùtóng de sīwéi hé gǎnjué fāngshì.

脆骨：

就七個魄而言，這種煉金術轉變通常會導致一種我們很少意識到的黑暗，直到它已經分裂為我們，像墨水一樣，天鵝絨般，幾乎舒適。

這始於品嚐毒藥。

體驗情感很好。

當他們成為消費激情時，應該小心。

Cuìgú:

Jiù qī gè Pò ér yán, zhè zhǒng liànjīn shù zhuǎnbiàn tōngcháng huì dǎozhì yīzhǒng wǒmen hěn shǎo yìshí dào de hēi'àn, zhídào tā yǐjīng fēnliè wèi wǒmen, xiàng mòshuǐ yīyàng, tiān'éróng bān, jīhū shūshì.

Zhè shǐ yú pǐncháng dúyào.

Tǐyàn qínggǎn hěn hǎo.

Dāng tāmen chéngwéi xiāofèi jīqíng shí, yīnggāi xiǎoxīn.

On the Tasting of Poisons

"Baby's Breath":

It is said that we have three hún and seven pò.

The three hún spirits are lofty, the seven pò are stuck with the body. The Pò of the person is connected with these seven lesser "souls" and often conscripts them into its service.

That is, the seven pò are the Pò (魄)[137] in action. The seven pò are the Pò in form.

They are but the means to compel and to force, to move with urgency, and to coerce that a sickened Pò will use to get its way.

The seven emotions (qīqíng; 七情) are often likened to poisons by the followers of the Buddha.

They can become that, but emotions are just movements of qì within us.

If we can regulate them, they do not become the seven pò, set upon to destroy us.

"Brittle Bones":

What is wrong with poison, anyway?

The sage Shennong had to taste all of the plants in order to know

137 Often translated as "cloud soul."

which among them could be used to heal. This also meant he partook of poisonous plants.

Sometimes, poison is the cure.

"Baby's Breath":

And "wise" men make the worst ghosts of all!

We all of us live in a world soaked and sometimes sotted with emotion.

They are part of the alchemy both of humans and of ghosts, living and dead.

There is an important thing to know: Even the ghost can be guided to a different way of thinking and feeling.

Patience and compassion are the only path to be taken if you are to transmute the emotions which, when they are in harmony can nourish us and, when they are out of balance can poison us deeply.

"Brittle Bones":

People often assume that Alchemy is used in order to achieve some perfection, or to reach enlightenment.

There is also an estranged, sweet, Alchemy to death.

The first stage is usually decomposition.

The 18th hexagram of the *Yijing* tells us this: Deeply ingrained patterns require decomposition.

Even the spirits that we think are bound to body or earth still go through transmutation.

The emotions do not immediately become poisonous, and the poisons do not immediately create sickness of the pò spirits, although this is a beginning.

At the same time, the seven pò spirits do not immediately become ghosts. Though this, too, is a beginning.

This is all a matter of a dark Alchemy, which occurs not under the light of the moon or at the height of midnight.

It occurs in much more hidden spaces barely shown by the light in our eyes.

In the case of the seven Pò, this alchemical transformation often results in a darkness we are rarely aware of until it has already cleaved to us, ink-like, velvety, and nearly comfortable.

This begins with the tasting of the emotional poisons.

It is fine to experience emotion.

It is when they become consumptive passions that one should take care.

COMMENTARY

THE HEART (XĪN) *must* reign, for that is its natural position, and it must rein in, for that is its duty. Exclusion does not naturally fit within the realm of the Heart:

> By nature, man possesses blood and breaths, and a heart that allows knowledge. Grief as well as joy and elation as well as anger do not exist permanently in [it]; they are reactions to the incitement of objects. It is then that the art of the Heart (Xīn)… intervenes.[138]

If we are to accept our emotions as expressions of qì, how are they considered poisonous as a matter of course? That is, if the emotions are so intrinsically bound to our human experience, how do we see them as immediately deleterious?

In brief there is a distinction, encountered within both Daoist and Buddhist contexts that draws a sharp distinction between the internal experience of the emotions (*qingxing*) and the internal experience of the virtues. The first century *Baihu tongde lun* begins by laying out the major lines of distinction between these two components of the psyche.

> What is the nature of our emotional disposition (*qingxing*)? Our moral values (*xing*) represent an expression of yang, while our emotional urges (*qing*) are a transformation of yin. Human beings are born into this world as an amalgam of yin and yang, and thus contain within us five core virtues (*wuxing*) and six basic emotional urges (*liuqing*). The word for emotion, *qing* (情), contains within it the meaning of *jing* (静)—that which is supposed to remain tranquil and kept under wraps. The character for virtue, *xing* (性), on the other hand, contains the attribute

JOHN ANDERSON

138 From the *Liji* of Yueju, found in: Larre and Rochat de la Vallee, *Rooted in Spirit*, 47.

226

sheng (生)—that which is meant to grow and reveal itself. Thus, the *Goumingjue (Secrets for Unifying the Forces of Life)* states:

All emotional turmoil is born from yin, and it is from here that obsessive impulses arise in waves; all sense of virtue is born from yang, and it is here where the drive toward a life of cultivation hails from. The momentum of yang is by nature compassionate, while the energy of yin is suffused with greed. That is why the emotions are at their core selfish and agenda-ridden, while the virtues are by nature selfless and full of compassion.[139]

The Pò is a dense spirit. It is a tremendously reactive part of our composite psyche, and one that is given to as well. As such, it can be thrown into disharmony quite easily if conditions are right. If the Pò is healthy, it can help us to digest, to discern, to disassemble, and to eliminate with decisive action and in a timely fashion. If it is unhealthy, it can cause stagnation and compartmentalization, if not outright dissociation from the body. Even as it is volatile, the Pò is absolutely necessary in order for us to incarnate.

The emotions are perhaps one of the most expedient ways that the Pò can become hardened, and, because we experience them every day, they are one of the hardest aspects of existence for each of us to change, akin to drying oneself while in the middle of a raging storm.

The Effect of the Emotions on Qì.

The seven emotions (qīqíng; 七情) recognized in Chinese culture are: anger, joy, sadness, grief, oppression, fear, and rumination. Each of these is said to affect specific aspects of the mind and are also considered the first step in most forms of disease. As one adage says: "All disease comes from the heart."[140]

139 Ban Gu, "On Humanity's Emotions and Higher Virtues: A Passage from the Chapter 'Qingxing' in the 'Baihu tongde lun' (Discussions on the Power of Virtue in the White Tiger Hall." Translated by Heiner Fruehauf, 2015: https://classicalchinesemedicine. org/humanitys-emotions-higher-virtues-passage-chapter-qingxing-baihu-tongde-lun-discussions-power-virtue-white-tiger-hall-ban-gu/ [Last accessed 30 Nov 2020].

140 Heiner Fruehauf, "All Disease Comes From the Heart: The Pivotal Role of the Emotions in

It should be underscored, however, that emotions are considered a natural expression of the human psyche, and that emotions, feelings, and affectations are considered to be manifestations of qì which have been refined, for better or for worse; they are also each said to affect the overall qì movement within the body in distinct ways. In this way, they are recognized as the "internal" cause of disease or disharmony.[141]

Anger causes the qì to rise.

Fear causes the qì to sink.

Sadness/Grief causes the qì to dissipate.

Rumination causes the qì to gather and stagnate.

Shock causes the qì to scatter.

Joy causes the qì to slow.[142]

What are the ramifications to these movements and accumulations of qì? In short, the qì and the blood cannot course smoothly, and the spirits cannot be carried. If there is slowing or stagnation of qì, the Shén become stuck in place. If there is dissipation of qì the Shén spirits, likewise, will have no medium to move in, much like a fish out of water, and at the least, will still be paralyzed. At worst, if this dissipation persists or is sufficiently jarring, it can also begin to consume

Classical Chinese Medicine" (2007): www.classicalchinesemedicine.org [Last accessed on 6 Dec 2020].

141 Giovanni Maciocia, *Foundations of Chinese Medicine: A Comprehensive Text, 3rd Edition* (London: Churchill-Livingstone, 2015), 257-65; For a more nuanced analysis of the role of the emotions on the internal milieu, including their effects on the interpersonal manifestations of qì, see Hammer, *Dragon Rises, Red Bird Flies*.

142 This attribution is found in many sources, but does not conform to the conditions generally implicated with an "excess" of joy (i.e., palpitations, manic behavior, insomnia, etc.). In my experience, excessive joy dissipates qì in an upward and outward manner. One can make the case that 'slowing the qì' is an outcome of chronic dissipation of qì. One can see this in the fatigue commonly felt by those who have gone through an extended bout of mania.

some of the denser aspects of the Shén spirits by consuming the jīng which gives individual shape to them and which also roots them.

As one of the more ineffable forms of qì, the emotions can become infixed in the same way that lactic acid and extra-cellular material can become an adhesion or a contusion within the layers of the skin and flesh; and just as physical scar tissue can build as a response to physical trauma, so too, traumatic events can give rise to psychic scars which will manifest in changes to emotional potentials, either as an overall blunting of the emotions, or as a state of hyper-reaction, as we encountered in the opening lines of this passage.

This is the environment which gives rise to the seven subordinate pò spirits mentioned earlier. If this state remains unresolved, the seven pò will begin to work of their own limited accord.[143] Each, then, begins to change the colour of one's emotions in ever-so-subtle ways until the field of emotional experience is transformed.

The trouble comes when the emotions begin to fester. When one's internal life begins to affect one's relation with other parts of oneself or others, this is when they begin to take on a poisonous quality.

The Embodiment

To find ease in the emotions, begin with living harmoniously with the quarters and the Seasons. The *Zhuangzi* tells us: "They (The Genuine Humans)[144] were cool like the autumn, warm like the spring, their joy and their anger intermingled with the four seasons" (Zhuangzi 6.1).[145]

Emotions are natural expressions of qì in given situations at given times. They are not necessarily "evil" or "negative" in themselves, even as codified religions and spiritual traditions try to make them so. They are part of lived experience.

---

143 This is somewhat analogous to the Jungian idea of the emotionally tinged "complex" which is seen by many as being semi-autonomous and as having some limited agency. In this case, the pò are seen as autonomous entities, and are thus afforded even more freedom.to affect the lives of host and perhaps even their lineage through time.

144 The term zhenren, ("True Person" or "Genuine Person") refers to one who is centered and authentic in their approach to themselves and others in the world. One who has both realized and embraced their Human nature, and who acts from this stance.

145 Brook Ziporyn, *Zhuangzi: The Complete Writings* (Cambridge: Hackett, 2020), 54.

A peace of mind follows from this realization, if it is sincerely grasped from the beginning.

They are only a movement of qì.

If the emotions are movements and manifestation of qì, also consider this:

The great poet Dufu advises us to "...[a]sk an unhappy ghost, throw poems to him..."[146]

A ghost is one who is caught in time, tied by knotted feelings, and by intense experiences relived. In order to step away from these oft-unwanted returns, the emotions and the affects must be moved, transmitted, or transformed.

How does one begin to affect change here?

Acknowledgment and Representation

To write, to tell—this is one way to transmute the poison to cure. But first, one should know the emotion that is being felt. When these are strong enough, these emotions lead to passion, and it is the passion that becomes the poison. Find in your own narrative some situation which holds you fast.

How are your emotions coloring the story of you? That is, do your emotions tinge the world a shade darker (Yin) or brighter (Yang) than it seems to be for others.

Is it consistent?

What causes you to feel stuck? What is the "feeling" of this, the immediate experience of being stuck?

Find external expression for the emotions that are felt, that in many cases that are held within. But do so in a way that restructures them, which shakes them to the core.

Anger becomes transformed once it is represented, once it is expressed. It is not only the "unwanted" emotions that are subject to this transmutation over an abyssal threshold from potential into being.

JOHN ANDERSON

146 Witter Bynner, (Trans.), "To Li Bai at the Sky's End," from *300 Tang Poems*, (New York: Knopf, 1920), 110.

Expression and Transmutation

Expression is vital. Allow yourself the immediacy and intensity of the emotion and the experience which accompanies it if it is safe to do so. In many cases this precipitates or is encouraged by secondary action. A bellow for its own sake can be a valuable release of pent up qì. Dance or other exercise and visual or musical composition also provide means by which to experience the rawness of burdensome or overwhelming emotions. Awareness of one's emotional states is the first step, here. That is, one must recognize and experience the emotions (though not always act on them), without clinging to them or "storing" them. It is the storage and "rotting" of emotion and other attendant experience that is harmful.

One such technique involves the use of emotion to control emotion, according to the Five Phases and is based on the "controlling cycle." It does not seek so much to "transform" emotions as such. Rather, it uses emotion to restrain emotion[147] in the following manner:

Sadness can treat anger: one must move the [client] with sad, painful and bitter words.

....[E]uphoria [Joy] can treat sadness: one must entertain the [client] with jokes, wisecracks, and practical jokes.

...[F]ear can treat euphoria: one must frighten the [client] with threatening words about death or bad luck.

...[A]nger can treat thought: one must provoke the [client] with insolent words.

147 In one sense, this may seem counterintuitive, but this approach seems aimed at addressing the emotion in the moment, and may be useful in preventing the emotions from becoming "poisonous" in the first place by providing more immediate recognition and expression.

...[T]hought can treat fear: one must divert the [client's] attention towards another subject, so that he forgets the cause of his fear. [...][148]

While this approach centered on a paired therapeutic encounter, the individual can affect similar change if they are consistent and aware within the practice.

Another key is the transformation or transmutation of the emotions themselves.[149]

To this end, the peasant-saint Wang Fengyi (1864–1937) also developed and implemented another, perhaps more nuanced methodology for transforming emotions based on Five Phase correspondences. The goal of this system is that it encourages one to embody more fully the five Confucian virtues which were the basis both of personal and social happiness, and which also allowed one to maintain one's overall health and identity within this system of healing.

The Shanren Dao

Wang Fengyi utilized a system of emotional counterbalance based on the enactment of the virtues and powers of the phase corresponding to the emotion gripping the individual. While it is true that the emotions are gradient manifestations of qì, they tend, when one is out of harmony with self and others, to cause a cascade of other, more malicious consequences. As with the Pò transmuting and transmitting the subordinate seven Pò mentioned above, the movement of the emotions could become poisons which were to be recognized and dealt with in a literal sense.

The approach called for the more Yin "poison" emotions to be uprooted and removed from the body in order that Yang qì could replace the heavy, stagnant feelings which mark these "poisons."

JOHN ANDERSON

148 Eliza Rossi, *Shen: Psycho-emotional Aspects of Chinese Medicine* (London: Elsevier, 2007), 31.
149 There are further ramifications of the emotions for the subtle architecture of the person (i.e., the collective Shén, and the nouome more generally). Much of this will be addressed in a subsequent volume.

The Five Poisonous Emotions

The Five Poisonous expressions of emotion[150] and their correspondences are as follows:

Hatred (Hèn; 恨) pertains to the Fire Phase and clings to the Heart (Xīn)

Irritation (Nǎo; 惱) pertains to the Metal Phase and clings to the Lungs

Anger (Nù; 怒) pertains to the Wood Phase and clings to the Liver

Annoyance[151] (Fán ;怒) pertains to the Water Phase and clings to the Kidneys

Blame (Yuàn; 怨) pertains to the Earth Phase and clings to the Spleen

In a manner similar to the correspondences laid out earlier for the "poisonous" expressions of emotion, within this system, each of these Phases align to specific "positive" internal states, or more precisely, expressions of virtue as Yang which are useful in controlling unwanted emotional states as Yin.

The Five Virtues

The Five Virtues stand as bulwarks against the volatility of the emotions and their propensity to color the internal experience. The Five Virtues are both concepts of action within the world *and* as modes of right-being within the world. That is, virtues are both active stances

---

150 Liu, *Let the Radiant Yang Shine Forth*, 5.

151 Also, vexed or troubled in a non-descript sense. Also may denote someone who is vaguely troubling to others. In the introduction to *Letting the Radiant Yang Shine Forth*, Heiner Fruehauf provides "disdain" as an additional gloss for this term. There is a reserved connotation to this term, indicating that it is often "hidden" in plain view. This implies not merely annoyance, but something more pervasive. "Contempt" may be another possibility here.

in relation to the world and underpinning states of existence.[152] Their corresponding associations are as follows:

PROPRIETY (LǏ; 禮)
Pertains to the Fire phase and expresses through the Heart.
Propriety is the capacity to recognize and act upon behavior which is appropriate for a given setting and time. Here, there is the idea of etiquette, "tact," and being able to hold one's attention and tongue where appropriate.[153]

EMPATHY (RÉN: 仁)
Pertains to the Wood phase and expresses through the Liver.
This is the capacity for compassion[154] and humane behavior toward other beings.

SOFTNESS/HARMONY[155] (RÓU/HÉ; 柔/和)
Pertains to the Water Phase and expresses through the Kidney
Rou/he is a quality of personal carriage or comportment. It calmness of demeanor and action as well as an openness or agreeableness which often accompanies this level of calm and ease in the world.

INTEGRITY/TRUSTWORTHINESS (XÌNSHÍ信實)
Pertains to the Earth Phase and expresses through the Spleen
This term includes ideas of constancy in emotion, experience, and consistency in action.[156]

JOHN ANDERSON

152 See Joseph Adler, "Zhu Xi's Spiritual Practice as the Basis of his Central Philosophical Concepts" (2008). His essay lays out the foundational process of the Song dynasty philosopher which is rooted both in the Yin/Yang dynamism found in Daoism and in the processional virtue of Confucianism. Zhuxi himself is widely considered the foremost proponent of "Neo-Confucian" ideals in light of this.

153 By extension, this also implies that one should have a sense of when one has a responsibility to speak or act even as others remain passive or quiet.

154 Considered the most Human of qualities. It is Rén that the Weeping Buddhas and Marys are reflecting to us.

155 Other commentators list "wisdom" as the virtue associated here, with softness/harmony being illustrative of the virtue of wisdom.

156 This virtue includes such related concepts as consistency and following through on one's word.

RIGHTEOUSNESS (YÌ; 義)

Pertains to the Metal Phase and expresses through the Lung
Righteousness is the quality of being upright in one's relations to other beings. This is doing the "right" thing by others and society in general. This term tends also to encompass ideas of fairness and justice.[157]

Virtue as Act

No event takes place in a vacuum, and for virtue to be of value, it must
be actionable. That is, one must find performative action if one is to
find virtue:

> To practice xiào (孝),[158] to its fullest, we cannot only rely on
> what our mouths speak but must follow up with action. Dao is
> expressed in actions. Dé (virtue; 惪) is something that you do. If
> you don't act on it, you don't have Dao, if you don't do things,
> you don't have Dé.[159]

The movement and change in emotions and emotional patterns
comes in changes to lived behavior. This change is initiated by the
Shén spirit of the Heart-mind in accordance with the Dao.

Thus, approaching the Shén in a way of virtue reigns. You must
approach yourself, and the Shén with a "firmness of purpose." All
change will cascade from this first internal movement.

One method to affect this change is a chant used in the Shanren
Dao system, which like so much else in the Chinese folk tradition

---

157 As mentioned in an earlier passage, "upright behavior" is not the same as being "self"-
righteous. Upright behavior is acted upon, with little need for an audience. Self-righteous
behavior tends to be spoken about first, and done only after. This does not imply that one
ought to act lawfully out of necessity. An unjust law should be challenged, and at times
broken, if it restores to oneself and others the ability to exist with clarity and openness and
does not restrict the means of others to do the same. This is holding oneself in equanimity
with others; "Selflessness" is another translation for "yi." This translation would also
indicate a quality of self-sacrifice.

158 This is a reference to virtue enacted within the family. In the Confucian tradition, one
should act in certain ways toward spouses, elder and younger blood relatives, as well as
work and social relationships.

159 Liu, *Let the Radiant Yang Shine Forth*, 128.

follows the Five Phase cycle in the "promoting" form.[160] It takes the form of a call-and-response in which one asks oneself

"Do I have/possess [x]?"
Each should then answer with an unequivocal
"Yes! I have/possess [x]?"

WOOD:

老善人看我有主意？

我有注意！

LĂO SHÀNRÉN KÀN WŎ YŎU ZHŬYÌ?

WŎ YŎU ZHŬYÌ

This chant cleanses anger and affirms zhǔyì 主意 ("firmness of purpose"), direction and motivation of the life force and boundless compassion.

FIRE:

老善人看我明理？

我明理！

LĂO SHÀNRÉN KÀN WŎ MÍNG LǏ?

WŎ MÍNG LǏ

This chant cleanses hatred and affirms mínglǐ 明理 ("illumination of the heavenly principle"), sacred connection, deep politeness, gratitude. Seeing the light of spirit in everything.[161]

These chants are of real value insofar as they reaffirm in the individual the conviction to live with virtue, but it should be reiterated that action (even in the form of inaction) is necessary for the truest expression of virtue to shine forth from the singular Shén as the spirit responsible for taking in and pouring forth experience.

---

160 The promotion cycle of the Five Phases is as follows: (Wood à Fire à Earth à Metal à Water à) at the end of one cycle, it begins anew with the newness and freshness inherent in the Wood Phase.

161 Each of the remaining phases has a similar form. The full cycle of chants will be examined in a subsequent volume wherein their specific effect on the Shen spirits can be more fully explored.

These chants reinforce the recognition that one's inner experience has the inchoate and embedded capacity for change (i.e., "I can and must transform something with me"), but they do so by asserting that one *already has what is needed.* These capacities have only been obscured by the Yin components of the nououme, which include the poisonous emotions and the psychic inertia which so often tends to accompany them.

Within this system, there must also be a visceral, heartfelt, and truthful response from the body itself. That is, in order for them to be moved or transformed, the emotions must be felt "in the gut," so to speak, which must be "evacuated" if one is to fully experience healing, clarity, depth, and freedom. This deeply embodied emotional response triggers a deep physical response, which reinforces the profound movement of qì that the system is meant to trigger. It is very much a psychosomatic system of healing, wherein we are asked to recognize, feel, and viscerally release the more "poisonous" expressions of our emotions.

All experience is a manifestation of qì, and the Daoist strives to avoid absolute preference or avoidance of any thing—even the more undesirable aspects of our own inner lives. Like the Divine Farmer Shénnong who tasted each herb to find the medicine and the toxin, we too must, partake of the poison if we are to have the salve, but as it was with Shénnong, the poison and cure are largely in the dose.

Do not forget this.

With regard to the work of the emotions, poisonous or numinous as they may be, the work is yours to do. No one can make you transform your qì. No one can do it for you. Others might give you a key, but you must go through the threshold. You are the only person that can transform your qì.

Even as considerable space has been devoted to Five Element correspondences for the emotions and the poisons which they might bring, remember that the Shén of the Heart is the one who will bear the brunt of existence in any long-term sense, and just as "ghosts are borne in the heart," the Shén spirits have their beginning in the Heart as well. The ghost must rewrite the poems which tell the story of its heart, if it is to transform itself to Shén.

To Be Humane

The *Zhuangzi* gives one last point of reflection regarding the emotions:

> Joy and anger,
>
> Sorrow and happiness,
>
> Plans and regrets,
>
> Transformations and stagnations,
>
> Unguarded abandonment and deliberate posturing—music flowing out of hollows, mushrooms of billowing stem!
>
> Day and night they alternate before us, but no one knows whence they sprout.[162]

Even to the sagacious, the emotions are an unknowable part of human existence, and the emotional life is one which can have perhaps the greatest impact on the unfolding of life. Recognizing and feeling and relating and regulating. This work with the emotions is something which we all can do, indeed must do if we are to avoid the poisons that the emotions can bring with them, but it takes work, effort, and time to do so.

162 Ziporyn, *Zhuangzi: The Complete Writings*, 10.

JOHN ANDERSON

脆骨：

我的血液是沉精神，通途和票價本身的通道和樹脂。

Cuìgú:

Wǒ de xiěyè shì chén jīngshén, tōngtú hé piào jià běnshēn de tōngdào hé shùzhī.

稚子气概：

當騎手隨著坐騎移動時，精神隨血液移動。

這是和平與一致的方式。

Zhìzǐ Qìgài:

Dāng qíshǒu suízhe zuòjì yídòng shí, jīngshén suí xiěyè yídòng.

Zhè shì hépíng yǔ yīzhì de fāngshì.

On the Keeping of One's Blood

"Brittle Bones":

My blood sits thickened in my veins.

It is condensed and full of qì, yet only moves when it is time.

The sap of a tree rises and falls in its due course, and thus they live for hundreds of years.

My blood is the throughway and the resin of my Shén spirts, the thoroughfare and the fare itself.

"Baby's Breath":

The spirits move with the blood as a rider moves with its mount.

This is the way of peace and accordance.

COMMENTARY

EVEN IN MODERN Chinese medical circles, lip service is paid to the connection between the blood[163] and the qì. The classics of Chinese medicine will tell the reader that the qì leads the blood and the blood carries the qì. While this statement is somewhat correct in its meaning, it does not capture the deeper stratagems at play within the body. Blood in its deeper meaning is the sum of the physical substrate of plasma, infused with the qì manufacture within and then further apotheosized by the presence of the Shén.

Here again, it is said that the blood does not become Blood until it has gone through the heart. Why? It is because the Xīn is the point of manifestation. It is here that the spirit of the Heart crosses over into embodiment. In order that the blood should become Blood, imbued as it is with the capacity for accepting and further as an abode of the spirits, the blood must first receive the sacrament of the Shén by passing through the Xīn, only to leave again instantly so that it can carry the qì and the shén with resoluteness, endurance, strength, and speed. The direct importance of this is that, for the Shén, that Vermillion Spirit which resides in the Heart, who finds a correlate in the Red Bird of the southern celestial and terrestrial quadrate, the Blood exists as a prerequisite for consciousness and conscious actions. There is, in the Blood, a clarity of awareness of the present-as-being. The rhythmicity of the Blood and of the Heart ultimately proves the blood[164] as substance in order that it may become Blood as carrier for consciousness and the Shén spirits, and it is, in fact, the Shén spirit which imparts this esoteric capacity to the Blood, and one

163 The concept of the blood is a complex set of ideas in many Asian cultures. It is not only the fluid medium within the circulatory system, it is further a quickened substance. For our purposes Blood, as the quickened substance is , it is inseparable from qì and it is the means upon which the qì moves and is carried throughout the body.

164 In Chinese medicine, the physical substrate of the blood is said to become Blood in its numinous form once it has transited through the Heart for the first time, during which time it is imparted with the "divine imperative" of the Shén.

can likewise nourish the Shén through working the Blood. The 26th chapter of the *Huangdi Neijing Suwen* emphatically states:

> The fact is, for nourishing the spirit, one must know whether the physical appearance is fat or lean and whether the [ying and wei qì],[165] the blood and the [jīng] qì,[166] abound or are weak. Blood and qì, [they are] the spirit of man; it is essential to nourish them carefully.[167]

Conversely, when the state of the Blood is not in good order and is not moving in a harmonious fashion cognition, memory, and concentration are very often affected.[168]

The present awareness and the presence-in-awareness are of primary importance here. Present awareness is the ability to observe and conceive of the world in a clear, unfettered way such that we are able to "see" what is occurring in the world, while also having awareness of our own biases which might affect these perceptions.

Awareness is seeing the world clearly, and presence-in-awareness is the ability to act upon the world from this state. These require a calmness, clarity, and ease of movement within the milieu of the Blood, both as substance and background for potential change and growth.

Further still, presence-in-action is the observation and experience of oneself as "sinking into" a relaxed state of "flow" wherein action is accomplished with minimal effort. This first requires an awareness of presence.

In this way, one of the most yin substances within the body is also one of the most yang.

JOHN ANDERSON

165 Translated by Unschuld as "camp" and "guard" qì, respectively, these indicate the interplay between inner and outer milieus of the body, both of which can affect the mind and the spirits as well as physical form.
166 This is the functional qì, which circulates through the vessels.
167 Unschuld, *Huang Di nei jing su wen*, 443; A more spirit-focused approach to the Blood as a carrier of spirit "power" will be revisited in a subsequent work. For now, it should suffice to say that the Blood, once it has passed through the Heart (Xīn) becomes the "carrier" of consciousness, and the "substrate" of awareness.
168 Maciocia, *The Foundations of Chinese Medicine*.

The Embodiment

The state of the Blood dictates the states of the mind, body, and the spirits, and it is well worth the time and effort to recognize and even become aware of the vital substances coursing through each of us, and the Blood is no different, and is most broadly covered by acts of "minding the blood" as an observational practice and actions aimed at "nourishing the blood."

Minding the Blood

The practice of keeping, that is nourishing and safeguarding the blood, is found in many cultures. The first step in embodied practice was mentioned above in the passage addressing seeing the world clearly and with all of the senses. The first step in any of the practices laid out here is awareness, but in this context, the reader is asked to observe the state of the blood through the observation of the pulsation of veins, arteries, and even capillaries as they distribute the blood into and across the body. This will also be a starting point for witnessing the coming and going of our own indwelling spirits. There are many ways to approach this practice, but one of the easiest is to take a bath.

Situate yourself in a tub of water that is comfortable and heated to your tolerance. If possible, lie back, submerging the back of the head to the point at which the ears are underwater, while the eyes and nose are still above the water level.

Concentrate on the chest as you begin to recognize the accentuated beating of your heart.

Next, attend to the sound of the blood as it moves through you.

Are you able to hear the Blood as it beats in your ears?

Do you notice pulsations at your fingertips?

As you are practicing this state of awareness, notice whether there are pronounced changes in rhythm or rate of the heartbeat as you inhale and exhale.

Practice this, and over time, you will become attuned to the "sound" of your heart as blood suffuses the tissues of the ears. It is when this sound becomes drastically unsteady that the spirits often will become, restless or even erratic.

Caring for the Blood

In order to do its work as courser and carrier, the Blood must be "fed." It must be maintained in the proper manner and, like any steed,[169] this includes both nourishment and movement.

To nourish the Blood is to provide it with the raw materials, the basic substances needed to for the body to produce the physical fluid medium of the blood. There is a process by which the interconnected matrix which is the blood must be formed so that the spirits and the qì might travel on, in, and with it. In Eastern culture this is most commonly achieved through diet, with herbal formulæ (of which many of the ingredients are foods themselves) are used to supplement if necessary.

When blood moves, there is life.

Here, then, we find another component of keeping the blood. That is, movement is necessary for the healthy creation and composition of the Blood. When the blood does not move, or does not move freely, it catches, congeals, and stagnates.

Given that movement is vital to the health of the blood as physical substance and Blood as a subtler carrier of consciousness, physical movement is also an essential component of keeping one's blood in a spritely state. To this end, mild to moderate exercise of nearly any sort will do wonders. The benchmark should be to work to a very mild sweat which stays on the skin and a slight increase in heartbeat and breathing.

Fatigue and shortness of breath here indicate overwork which has served to sap function (i.e., the qì) and form (i.e., the blood).

Even here at this relatively gentle stage, be aware of the changes taking place.

JOHN ANDERSON

---

169 In this case, the Blood is the "steed" of the Shén spirits, and the mover of qì. In Chinese medicine, there is the dictum "Qì commands the Blood, Blood carries the qì."

Returning to the topic of nourishment, we should understand blood as being a rich, dense substance, and as such it requires rich, dense materials to fortify it. One of the representative formulæ for nourishing the Blood is Huánglián Ējiāo Tang (*Coptis* and Gelatin Decoction).[170] It is a formula which contains many of the ingredients used for "building blood" as well as moving or "coursing" the blood and, when necessary, also calming the Shén spirit.

The ingredients in Huánglián Ējiāo Tang include:

Báisháoyào (Peony; 白芍药)

Ējiāo (Gelatin; 阿胶)[171]

Huánglián (*Coptis*; 黄连)

Huángqín (*Scutellaria baicalensis*; 黄芩)

Jīzǐhuáng (Egg yolk: 鸡子黄)[172]

Ējiāo, Báisháoyào, and Jīzǐhuáng (if it is included) are useful in promoting Yin, which is vital in the formation of the physical substrate of blood.

Included within the structure of this formula, we also encounter ingredients that serve to maintain consistent movement of the blood within the vessels.

170 This formula was included in the *Shanghan Lun (Treatise on Cold Damage)* written by Zhang Zhong Jing during the Eastern Han dynasty (220 bce to 206 ce).
171 Within this formula, the Ejiao (gelatin) can be replaced with substances such as Di Huang (*Radix rehmannia*) if there are dietary or ethical concerns, though it will change the alchemy of the formula to some extent to do so.
172 As with gelatin, this can be omitted if there are dietary or ethical concerns. It bears consideration though, that, as in many cultures, like nourishes like, and to take out an animal product is to weaken the qì of the formula. Even where plants are concerned, the essence extracted from them is likened to blood and the work of preparation directly takes the qì of the plant, up to the point of killing it. It is true, then, in this case that herbal preparation is a violent, even murderous, business.

The ability of a substance to course, or move, the blood allows rich materials to help create the richness of blood without promoting an environment of stagnation which can often characterize such rich ingredients.

Lastly, the formula includes ingredients such as huánglián (coptis) and huángqín (scutellaria) which both serve to "clear Heat,"—an aspect of pathology which can over-stimulate the Shén spirits and the Heart as the abode of the singular Shén, which, in turn, gives rise to agitation.

Huanglian Ejiao Tang is thus a representative formula for creating and moving blood as a means toward calming the Shén spirit, itself a vital component of the formation of the energetic and spiritual aspects of Blood. It is the herbal correlate to the flight of the Red Bird to the South.

Other formulæ which might be suitable include Shengmai San (Generate the Pulse Powder),[173] or Danggui Sini Tang (Tangkuei Four Frigid Limbs Decoction) if the Blood must be conserved or fortified through herbal means.

Overall, nutrition is one of the most understated aspects of keeping the blood. Anemia, as a Western medical condition, is most implicated as being a malady of the blood. The correlates in most traditional Asian medicines are *qixu* and *xuexu* (deficiency of vital function and deficiency of "blood," respectively), both of which can manifest as fatigue, lack of motivation, and cognitive deficits as well as a dullness of countenance or "spirit." See the passage "On Nutrition" in the present work for greater context.

To Be Humane

The Blood is the physicalized interaction of the Yin and Yang. The conjoining of these principles precludes any aspect of animal life, and human life is the same. When the Blood is kept well, nourished and moved, there is Tai (peace or accordance) such that Heaven and Earth

173 This formula does not address the Blood directly. Its ingredients serve to strengthen and protect the functional qì of the Heart (Xīn), which is necessary for the vitalized form of Blood to be constituted in the body.

are fully realized.[174] This can be seen as something that separates human beings from other aspects of the world, but this is illusory, at best. The blood suffuses each of us, in this we are no different than other members of the animal kingdom. The humaneness of this is the simultaneous recognition that the blood, mundane and common to all, is also the Blood, a marvel of vitalized reality, which empowers each of us as individuals.

174 This is the image provided by the 11th hexagram of the *Yijing*. It consists of three broken lines above three solid lines. The state intimated here is one of ease and naturalness. The Yin and Yang are linked in their proper manner in this hexagram as the Yang buoys the Yin, and the Yin anchors the Yang.

稚子气概：

鬼魂對精神有不同的意義，並以千種不同的方式
展現在人體中。

Zhìzǐ Qìgài:

Guǐhún duì jīngshén yǒu bùtóng de yìyì, bìng yǐ qiānzhǒng bùtóng de fāngshì zhǎnxiàn zài réntǐ zhōng.

脆骨：

鬼魂和惡魔將盡力駐紮在每一個心中。

知道為什麼要讓它們越過門並越過閾值，但不要
讓它們失控。

Cuìgú:

Guǐhún hé èmó jiāng jìnlì zhùzā zài měi yī ge xīnzhōng.

Zhīdào wèishéme yào ràng tāmen yuèguò mén bìng yuèguò yùzhí, dàn bùyào ràng tāmen shīkòng.

稚子气概：

沉公知道鬼是一種奇怪的意識，

或意識改變了

或疏遠的"在那裡"。

在某種程度上，久違的表親。

Zhìzǐ Qìgài:

Chén gōng zhīdào guǐ shì yīzhǒng qíguài de yìshí,

huò yìshí gǎibiànle

huò shūyuǎn de "zài nàlǐ".

Zài mǒu zhǒng chéngdù shàng, jiǔwéi de biǎo qīn.

脆骨：

記得在"鬼魂"世界中成為沈神的守護者。

自由而清晰，因此您將按原樣看到事物。

Cuìgú:

Jìdé zài "guǐhún" shìjiè zhōng chéngwéi chén shén de shǒuhù zhě.

Zìyóu ér qīngxī, yīncǐ nín jiāng àn yuányàng kàn dào shìwù.

On Ghosts

"Baby's Breath":

Ghosts are a difficult thing.

They can be dead, alive, or both.

Ghosts mean different things to the Shén spirits, and are shown in the body in a thousand different ways.

"Brittle Bones":

Ghosts and demons will try to lodge in every heart.

Know why you are letting them past your gate and across your threshold, but do not turn them away out of hand.

Unless you would treat all visitors in this manner.

In this case, you may be the ghost you are working so meticulously to avoid!

"Baby's Breath":

Work to transform ghosts (guǐ) into spirits (shén), and your work in every part of the world will be transformed.

The Xīn should solely be the abode of the Shén, but regard and compassion for the wandering beings is still given.

If they are granted this much room the eyes remain clear and the Xīn (heart-mind) moves smoothly and freely.

The Shén knows the guǐ as a strange awareness,

Or a changed awareness,

Or an estranged "there-ness."

Long-lost cousins, in a way.

"Brittle Bones":

But what is it, to be a ghost within the realm of the Xīn?

Regret unbidden?

Memories relived and not made new?

Master Dogen tells us that hungry ghosts see water as raging fire or pus and blood.[175]

Remember to be a keeper of Shén in a world of Ghosts.

Free and clear, thus you will see things as they are.

---

175 From Dogen, "Sansui Kyo" ("Mountains and Waters Discourse"). Translated by Kazuaki Tanahashi: https://www.upaya.org/uploads/pdfs/MountainsRiversSutra.pdf [Last accessed on 6 Dec 2020].

COMMENTARY

THE GHOSTS AND demons held deeply within the heart prevent or pervert the awareness of the world provided by the collective Shén and shown through by the singular Shén. The awareness is fundamentally and deeply changed when ghosts come to lodge within us. The purity of limpid running water will rise to one's eyes as flames or will fill the nostrils as so much feces to be full rejected—or ejected altogether.

Traditionally, this dynamic tends to put guǐ at odds with the broader, more rarified Shén, both human and non-human, found in the world. In a word, ghosts are not much more than unfulfilled spirits. This can be rectified, to a great extent, and indeed should be rectified, particularly where the shén of living persons is concerned. We are capable of profound change when we are alive, and it is this capacity for change which makes the transmutation of guǐ largely a human endeavor.

It is very often a matter of movement, and, in the same way that lack of movement can cause the qì to stagnate, so too, a diminution of "movement" of the Shén can lead one toward becoming guǐ.

Failure to do so brings more of the same, and over time can further insulate the guǐ against change.

There are many ways to approach the appearance and appeasement of guǐ as the term is most often glossed within the Chinese popular culture.

In the haunted world of early China, one approach was to transform ghosts into beneficial (one hoped) ancestors. Another was to claim that ghosts are, on the contrary, embedded in a moral pantheon that rewards the good and punishes the bad. Yet another approach was to seek to step outside such a process altogether—not worship ghosts, not become a ghost oneself—and instead seek some form of self-divinization.[176]

Auto-apotheosis is far beyond the scope of the present text, and in the present context, not altogether useful. What might be said is that one ought to live in accordance with the Shén if one wishes to live in accord with the Dao.

For further commentary on the ramifications of ghosts for the individual psyche, see also the passage entitled "Embracing the Ghost." The upshot for this text lies with the effect that muted awareness can have on an individual. Experience of life becomes blunted, and awareness becomes clouded. The Shén which resides in the heart stands in stark contrast to this.

Clarity and emptiness are the two main qualities quintessentially related to the Xīn, or Heart-mind. Experience of the world, as it is received by the singular Shén which is housed in the Xīn, the physicality of the heart, and evaluated therefrom, is the bona fide currency of life.

The Embodiment

We are composites of spirits working through each of us. Remember that most ghosts begin as Pò spirits which have become fractured, instinctual, and pained. A wounded animal. It affects nearly every aspect of bodily function, but very specifically, the functions of digestion and respiration. The bare biophysical processes necessary to keep us alive—this is the domain of the Pò.

When we talk about ghosts in this context, we mean living ghosts most specifically. They are still informed by biophysical function and the capacity for change and adaptation. Change and adaptation which must first surface in the process of awareness. Even this awareness can be ghostly, in a certain way.

JOHN ANDERSON

176 Michael Puett, "Sages, the Past, and the Dead—Death in the *Huainanzi*," in Amy Olberding and Philip J. Ivanhoe, (eds.), *Mortality in Traditional Chinese Thought* (Albany: SUNY Press, 2011), 225–49.

Ghosts often see the illusions that they wish to see. They reexperience the patterns that have held life. It is very difficult to teach an old ghost new tricks because its awareness so delimited, focused, and circumscribed.

This is why the Shén and the Guǐ (i.e., spirits and ghosts) are often placed in opposition to one another within the Chinese tradition. It is not because one is made of an inherently different stuff. The substance of spirits and of ghosts are remarkably similar. Rather, it is the way one interacts with awareness and with its own experience.

Since we are not talking about the cessation of biophysical life processes as an indicator of ghostly predisposition, we must enumerate what actually fits this predisposition. In the simplest terms, it is the dulling of awareness, the illusory worlds that the ghost creates, which qualify its being.

This can be further exacerbated by a lack of connection with and regard for others. We humans have need for connection to others which, if unmet, can leave us unfulfilled, stunted, or even hollowed.

The most chilling component of this form of isolation is that one becomes numb to the proposition that other beings, other agents exist in the world as anything more than extensions of the wants or needs of the ghostly individual.

The Urgency of Grief

In the earlier passage "On the Tasting of Poisons," a schema was laid out in which each of our Shén corresponds to one of five major emotional states. In that passage, the Pò is particularly susceptible to the overwhelming sense of emptiness, which we call grief. When it is immediate, grief tends to overshadow the other emotions. It does this by dampening our ability to create, utilize, and move qì. This applies at any point of being, and can account for such unwelcome guests as: lack of motivation, the stilted movement, and/or the diminished capacity for happiness or even anger. Even worse, perhaps, is its insidious effect on the human capacity for hope, this being one of the few things which might allow one to fully process the grief which the being[177] may be feeling.

Recognition and Expression

The embodiment herein rests on one's capacity to allow the loss to be fully expressed or embodied rather than repressed, shunted, and shut down. How an individual approaches this process can be as complex as writing a biography of a loved one, or as simple as full-throated crying or hot rage.

The first component of this is recognition that one is feeling. Grief tends to subdue the felt-sense of novelty over time. Not that one should not grieve, but that one should be mindful of the role that it plays and that over-exposure to grief can sap the ability to feel much else.

The next is that one release this as best one can. Grief takes the time that it takes, but grief should take on a different nature after a point. You may still long for a thing, you may still have a fondness for a person, but what you are being asked to dig into is the suffering experienced due to loss. The qualia of the experience is the mystery for each of us.

Failure to do this will often lead to attempts to quell pangs of grief that surface, all the while trying to hold the feeling in check. This is a dynamic that does not often last. Here comes the hunger which many living ghosts feel as they engage something as a means to feed the fallow void so often marks living ghosts, and which throws a heavy tapestry over the clarity provided by the brightness of the Shén.

Feeding Your Pò

Because the Pò is so heavily intertwined with ghosts which tend to reside within and around us, it is necessary to provide the Pò with extra attention. The Pò is a natural part of us, which will remain attached to

177 It has been thoroughly postulated at this point that other creatures experience something akin to grief, though it may be more a fond remembrance rather than a deep ache which marks this sort of experience. We may never know the true quality of it.

the Earth once we pass on, and which is prone to become a ghost as it is classically understood in the West.

Stemming from the Tibetan tradition, this practice translates roughly to "the rite of offering one's body" (Tib., *lus sbyin*),[178] and has been tranlated into a more contemporary practice known as "Feeding Your Demons" transmitted to the West by Lama Tsultrim Allione.[179] This method, asdapted from the Chod practices of the tantrika Machig Labdron (1055–1149 CE) this practice has an affinity for many types of restless, unwell, or unwanted beings, which are themselves illusory according to the Tibetan Chod tradition.

The broad strokes of this practice are extrapolated here so as to include the restless, dis-eased Pò of any person, particularly one that has begun to "separate" from the workings of the body and the other Shén in such a way that its autonomy counters the work of the body, the other collective Shén, or the person as a whole. These are signs that one is in the process of becoming ghost-like.

This practice asks the individual to dialogue with the "other" being, (in this case, the disquieted Pò[180]) in order to ask three seemingly simple questions:

- What do you want?
- What do you need?
- How would it feel if you got what you needed?

This is accomplished by setting out two seats. The person will ask the question as themselves from the first seat or space. They will then switch seats to the second seat and answer as the Pò. They will continue to do this with each question separately, moving back and forth as

---

178 Jerome Edou, *Machig Labdron and the Foundations of Chod* (Ithaca: Snow Lion, 1996).

179 Tsultrim Allione, *Feeding Your Demons: Ancient Wisdom for Resolving Inner Conflict* (New York: Little, Brown & Co., 2008).

180 It should be emphasized here that, while the Hún and the Pò both have connotations of autonomy or freedom of movement which the other collective Shén do not generally have, it is unnatural for the Pò to become "other," especially with regard to working against the individual to whom it is native. It can be seen as somewhat akin to "autoimmune" processes that can profoundly affect the physical milieu.

necessary. In doing this, they give room for the Pò, or a ghost, or a demon to have its own voice, its own representation, and its own space.

Once these questions have been answered fully, the person will switch back to the first seat and begin the process of feeding. In doing this, the person works to cultivate and then channel to the Pò, ghost, or demon that feeling which was indicated as feeling fulfilled. For example, if the Pò indicated that the feeling of quiet joy was the feeling that it would feel if its needs were met, the person would work to "flood" the other with the feeling of quiet joy, so that it would have the feeling of being fulfilled given to it, or as the name suggests, fed to it.

This is the point wherein the singular Shén will fulfil its utmost purpose as the arbiter of the Shén spirits. It is the numinous potential which must be incorporated, and it oversees the Divinity of the other forms. It is the spirit which "feeds" the Pò in this exercise. The Shén facilitates experience, awareness, and, in this case, nourishment. As the Dao tells us, it is the emptiness which allows for filling. The Shén provides what the Pò needs by asking and pouring out what the Pò is "missing."[181]

As you work with the Shén, feel the qì of the Xīn and singular Shén pouring into the Lungs, (the traditional abode of the Pò) as a clear bright light of a red hue. It might be "seen" internally as red flame or a red bird. As this qì ascends to the abode of the Pò, the "temperature" of the qì pouring forth from the Shén should become cooler as it rises into the chest and as the Pò takes it in.

Once the Pò has fully taken in the qì furnished by the Shén, the "color" and "feel" of the qì will also change. The qì will become lighter still as it mists up, becoming a clear "white" light which may be slightly tinged with other hues.

It is the clarity and lightness of the sensation, which is key here.

The caveat is that the process of feeding to true fulfillment can take a long time. In this case, many sessions of this sort may be neces-

JOHN ANDERSON

181 There are those who would assert that this idea of some missing potential or experience is illusory or inconsequential, but it is the draw for some unrealized process which leads most of us to pursue practices of cultivation of any sort, and in this sense, is necessary at some level. This friction underlies many of the themes found in this text

sary before the person and their native Pò can reach a point of equanimity, wherein the Pò again takes up its proper position within the individual so that both are able to flourish, change, and adapt.

To Be Humane

The utmost humanity hinted at in this passage is the clear and deeply felt pathos which comes from the recognition that each of us is perhaps only one or two steps away from ourselves becoming ghosts in a living sense. The upshot here is that *every* person that we will meet has had life events which could, under the right (or wrong) circumstances leave one less capable of embodying their destiny (Ming) had those events not occurred. In most cases, the person still has the capacity to "rebuild" themselves in new way. It is this capacity for returning to and rebuilding connection and experience which distinguishes a living ghost from a "true" human.

There is no person, regardless of spiritual path, who is immediately disqualified from this state of being, although it is true that some spiritual paths are better able to equip adherents with useful tools for avoiding this state. In truth, nearly any practice which is deeply held and sincerely embodied and which does not detract from another without their fully given informed consent can be something of a safeguard by providing a signpost and a beacon of the Human Way outlined here.

脆骨：

許多人有頭，

並且不要使用它們。

Cuìgú:

Xǔduō rén yǒu tóu,

bìngqiě bùyào shǐyòng tāmen.

稚子气概：

當頭部漂浮在上方時，幽靈可以從朦朧的距離看到世界，但是幽靈無法真正觸摸世界。

鬼角色的中心是一個字段。

與其他男人和女人聯繫在一起的耕地。田野既不能深耕，也不能完全收穫。

對於幽靈來說，正是它們所缺乏的：

營養。

營養，

光。

和其他人的命運。

Zhìzǐ Qìgài:

Dāngtóu bù piāofú zài shàngfāng shí, yōulíng kěyǐ cóng ménglóng de jùlí kàn dào shìjiè, dànshì yōulíng wúfǎ zhēnzhèng chùmō shìjiè.

Guǐ juésè de zhōngxīn shì yīgè zìduàn.

Yǔ qítā nánrén hé nǔrén liánxì zài yīqǐ de gēngdì. Tiányě jì bùnéng shēngēng, yě bùnéng wánquán shōuhuò.

Duìyú yōulíng lái shuō, zhèng shì tāmen suǒ quēfá de:

Yíngyǎng.

Yíngyǎng,

Guāng.

Hé qítā rén de mìngyùn.

On Reattaching the Head

"Brittle Bones":

Many ghosts do not have heads,[182]

And have no need of them.

Many humans have heads,

And further, do not use them.

And thus, are so many ghosts incubating.

"Baby's Breath":

I tell you,

There is a thin tether, this little neck, and the head of a ghost cannot stay attached.

It floats above the fields.

The fields of the earth become mottled brown paintings, which can be admired but never engaged.

---

182 Recall the commentary provided by Star as it was given in the earlies passage "Embracing the Ghost," which details the component parts of the Chinese character guĭ. In this passage, the theme is similar. As a ghost, one can easily lose their way and finds themselves "lost among the fields," or separated from the cultivated (i.e., "human") places. In addition, we can very easily lose connection with components of ourselves.

It floats above the villages and towns.

The gatherings of women and men become as flocks of brothers and sisters, to which they cannot belong.

It floats above the cities.

Greyed with the industries of men,

Bustle and distraction,

It is here wherein a ghost might find a place to alight,

But it will not belong.

This is the lament of the ghost.

What does it mean?

When the head floats above, the ghost can see the world from a hazy distance, but the ghost cannot truly touch the world.

The center of the character for ghost is a field. A cultivated space, which is connected with other men and women. Fields it can neither furrow deeply nor harvest completely.

For the Ghost it is these that it lacks:

Nourishment.

Nourishment,

Light.

And destiny among other people.

But it is not just this…

To keep one's head is to have the manifestation of coherence which takes its beginning from the heart (Xīn).

To have lost one's head is to be cut off from the Heart.

This the Shén spirits cannot abide.

They may stay for a little while,

But too much, and most will go.

Except the Pò.

It will stay—perhaps overlong.

Thus, a ghost of a different sort is birthed.

COMMENTARY

One of the lesser-known customs which was practiced (and presumably still is practiced) in some areas of China is that of wugu.[183] This sorcerous practice involves the creation and tending of an entity which would be unleashed on a victim. It may be done at the whim of the sorcerer for their own needs, though it was also undertaken at the behest of a client.

Its appearance was manifold, and its use widespread:

> It is…a thing which produces excessive indulgence in debauchery, as also disorders by confusion of the mind; in its written form it contains the components "pot" and "reptiles or insects," constituting the character ku; the flying insects in corn also are ku, and in the Cheu yih (the Yih king) a girl confounding a man, and the wind blowing down from the mountains are said to be due to ku;—all these matters are of the same kind[…][184]

Details varied, but often included the amalgamation and refinement of poisons through placing several venomous creatures into a vessel until only one remained. During this time, it was to be kept in a darkened place out of the sight of guests and other animals such as roosters or dogs.

The last surviving animal was said to retain the poisonous properties and venomous virtues and of each of the other animals which it had consumed while sealed within the vessel.

The nature of this entity varied. It was part physical creature and part malevolent spirit, after all, and its specific use varied from familial tradition to familial tradition.[185]

183 J. M. de Groot, *The Religious Systems of China: Its Ancient Forms, Evolution, History and Present Aspect. Manners, Customs and Social Institutions Connected Therewith*, Vol. 5, (Leiden: Brill, 1964); H. Y. Feng, and J. K. Shryock, "The Black Magic in China Known as K'u," *Journal of the American Oriental Society* 55.1 (1935): 1–30.
184 J. M. de Groot, *The Religious Systems of China*, 5:333.
185 The use of Gu could take on many forms. In some forms of Gu, the creature was seen

The main problem with this practice?

It was highly illegal in pre-Imperial and Imperial China. In *The Great Ming Code: Da Ming Lu*, Jiang Yong-Lin details the statute involving the care and illicit use of Gu poisons:

Article 312—"Killing Others by Making or Keeping Gu Du" (Zao Xu Gu Du Sha Ren)

[1] In all cases of making or keeping Gu poison that can be used to kill others or of training others [to make or keep gu poison, the offenders shall be punished by decapitation. The property of those who make or keep [Gu poison] shall be forfeit to the government...[186]

This extreme punitive response was an ancient one, dating to the Han Dynasty (202 BCE–220 CE).[187]

Decapitation and forfeiture of one's financial legacy were the punishments for participation in nefarious works of black magic and usury as embodied by Gu. Worse than this, however, was the subsequent existence which befell the carcist and those around them if he or she died in this gruesome manner.

You see, the Gu as a spirit needed to be fed and contained and was bound to the practitioner for these purposes. If the practitioner was unable to fulfil his or her side of the operation, there was the risk that the unkempt Gu spirit could reverse what magic it had performed on

as an amalgamated poison that was then introduced to food or drink so as to poison an individual. The perpetrator would then wait for the victim to die slowly (or to extract a desired outcome by providing an antidote to the poison once conditions were met. In other traditions, the Gu was a spirit servitor who would be bound in loyalty to the perpetrator of the Gu or the client of the Gu practitioner. According to de Groot, this servitor would do various activities, both mundane (i.e., cleaning the home) and supramundane (i.e., haunting one's neighbors) with the ultimate goal of maintaining or increasing the individual house and holdings of the practitioner or client.

186 Jiang Yonglin, *The Great Ming Code: Da Ming Lu* (Seattle: University of Washington Press, 2014), 172.

187 "Cheng K'ang-ch'eng's commentary on this passage in the Chou li quotes the criminal law of the Han dynasty as saying, 'Those who dare to poison people with ku, or teach others to do it, will be publicly executed.'" (Feng and Shryock, *The Black Magic in China Known as K'u*, 6).

behalf of the practitioner or client *and* if the practitioner was exposed keeping and using Gu, they ran the risk of themselves *becoming Gu spirits*,[188] floating above the world as disembodied heads in search of sustenance and a goal.

In the case of this passage, there is likely no capital crime committed by the person so affected, but the outcomes laid out above may be apropos.

One can easily view decapitation as a fair metaphor for traumatic experience visited upon one which can readily give rise to the bifurcated dynamic between the mind and body, and just as with the punitive characteristic mentioned above, there is the chance for loss of contact between the "rational" processes of the mind and the fully embodied presence of one's physicality. That is, with insult or trauma there is chance of disconnection with and diminution not only of mental capacities, but also a cleaving from the material needs of the body itself and the raw experiential potential which it provides.

If the previous passage outlines the Pò as the anchor of the ghostly impulse, this passage concerns the dissociation that can occur when we are, ourselves, haunted by the world.

A mind disconnected from the immediacies of the body often does little good over the long term. To be in one's head allows for a sharpness, a keenness of vision, which can become driven and it allows for the intellect to flourish in a sea of hard polarities. It can, however, also prevent the expression or experience of "softer," subtler, and more personal impressions, and also tends to thwart deeper connections with self and others. Both of these states are consistent with ghostly behavior. These characteristics do not mark one necessarily as a ghost, but they do indicate that there is a disconnect within the person. It is this essential disconnect which is at play here, and just as ghosts or spirits can float in the air if not called to heel by some method, the mind and the body can drift apart if not properly safeguarded.

To act with ease and spontaneity in the world, and to balance Yin and Yang is the goal of life according to Laozi and Zhuangzi. To do

188 The Han period *Shuowen Jiezi* also defines gu as "the spirits of convicted criminals whose heads had been exposed on stakes."

this, there must be a connection between one's intellectual capacities with the Heart-mind as well as the physicality of the body itself. These should all hopefully find purchase with one another as they were interconnected at birth.

As with so much else in this text, the importance of this situation lies with the play between Yin and Yang, or, more alarmingly, the lack thereof which has become a common trait in our constantly moving, if unengaged, world.

The Embodiment

In the previous passage we encountered the existential state of the ghost, and in this one, we come up against the fundamental disconnect which must be acknowledged and addressed if we are to return to the Human way.

Reestablish the interchange of Yin and Yang. To reattach the head is to promote communication between the lower spaces where the Pò resides and the upper spaces from which the Hún finds its comings and goings. Again, this shows physiologically as a tightness of being and is common. A great many of us in the West hold tension in the neck, shoulders, and jaw, areas, and if this condition is chronic, it will lead to postural entrainment which will serve to dam up one's energy and restrict the flow of the blood in the area.

Energetically, this tension and cutting off of one's felt sense at the throat and neck causes a separation between the head and the body, which may be as severe as a complete disassociation or as innocuous as a dulling of sensation and coordination.

The work in this passage is to reestablish connection between the head and the body through the jaw, neck, and shoulders. This is most easily accomplished by working to relax the jaw, neck, and shoulders even if only momentarily. Massage is one method, to be sure, but some may find it invasive or uncomfortable, particularly if they are overstimulated or if boundaries have been compromised by past experience. Hypervigilance and hyperreaction reign, in this case. Conversely, the tactile felt sense or the psychological connection to feeling itself may be muted. In this state, the person may not even feel the physical contact. The building of meaning is the operative process here. In this case, it is restraining or even retraining of embodiment itself.

Other examples of useful activity include any expressive movement process aimed at reestablishing awareness of the mind within the body. Dance, Yoga, and other low-impact sports are useful here, as they tend to keep awareness on the body. Martial arts may be useful to some extent, provided it is not too rigid or tight. The general goal is to remain relaxed so that qì and experience proceed naturally.

One of the easiest to rekindle this connection is to soak in water, to submerge and otherwise practice some form of cleansing of the body.

Float.

Be empty.

Notice how it "feels" to do both.

Both water and emptiness, when we are submerged in them, allow for an evenness in experience. Just as the water surrounds on all sides, seeping in and supporting us as we float, so too, the openness and evenness of internal emptiness can affect the Heart and Mind.

Many a good idea washes over us in the shower or the bath. A novel approach, a new point of view, or the opening lines of a new novel can all be found when the head is reconnected to the body.

Doing any of this does not preclude the rational. Rather it seeks to acknowledge the "knowledge" of the gut, and in so doing, to reestablish meaningful contact between the Hún and the Pò through awareness (i.e., through the work of the singular Shén).

To Be Humane

To reconnect the head, Heart, and Mind with the body is to reclaim the movement that is intrinsic to the human in order that they be in accordance with one's surroundings.

This allows one to move with "the great river" of the *Yijing*, recognizing chance encounters and enduring the inevitability of change inherent within life without becoming swept away by its current.

When we are well connected to our experience, we recognize in ourselves and in others the capacity for, indeed the necessity of change which culminates in our own mortality. The humanity inherent in this passage is one of reconnection. It speaks to the tenuous nature of connection to the many and varied parts of ourselves when we have had to run the gauntlet of life, so many poisonous things sealed in with us that cause us to lose connection both to ourselves and to others, which comes at the revelation of mortality, expressed as a life to be led.

稚子气概：

在另一條道路上，可以選擇清空以面對手頭的工
作，就像清空"心"一樣。

這項工作是道的人類運動。

這是一種生活。

這是明的追隨，是人類的方式。

這是空心的。

Zhìzǐ Qìgài:

*Zài lìng yītiáo Dàolù shàng, kěyǐ xuǎnzé qīngkōng yǐ miàn duì shǒutóu de
gōngzuò, jiù xiàng qīngkōng "xīn" yīyàng.*

Zhè xiàng gōngzuò shì dào de rénlèi yùndòng.

Zhè shì yīzhǒng shēnghuó.

Zhè shì míng de zhuīsuí, shì rénlèi de fāngshì.

Zhè shì kōngxīn de.

脆骨：

照顧那些無聊而不是無聊的人，因為即使道已經
很自私，我們也不知道。

我們的"稻草狗"仍然不過是道的表現。

要成為暴力的船隻或同情的載體，就需要火焰。

最好讓骨頭像鳥一樣空心，以便道的運作可以通
過。

Cuìgú:

*Zhàogù nàxiē wúliáo ér bùshì wúliáo de rén, yīnwèi jíshǐ dào yǐjīng hěn zìsī,
wǒmen yě bù zhīdào.*

Wǒmen de "dàocǎo gǒu" réngrán bùguò shì dào de biǎoxiàn.

Yào chéngwéi bàolì de chuánzhī huò tóngqíng de zàitǐ, jiù xūyào huǒyàn.

*Zuì hǎo ràng gǔtou xiàng niǎo yīyàng kōngxīn, yǐbiàn Dào de yùnzuò kěyǐ
tōngguò.*

On Being Hollow

"Baby's Breath":

To be hollowed is to have something taken from you which sustained you deeply or which is necessary for coherence of the Shén spirits, the Xīn, and body.

This is the beginning of two Paths—one must choose, lest the choice be made.

The first is marked by the beginning of dissonance and the incipience of separation between Yin and Yang.

How do you know when such a thing has happened?

When the face pales and grows numb, when the stomach becomes heavy, when the limbs grow cold, when the spirits have fled their internal abodes and take with them the light of the eyes, when begging hands and hungry mouths remain empty, when there is great noise, when there is fear of what the light will show or what the darkness hides, when harm comes to call upon oneself, and when the ghostly Pò is all that remains.

This is how one will know.

This is being hollowed.

This is the first step on the Path of the Living Ghost.

On another path, one can choose to be empty in order to face the work at hand, as in emptying the Heart.

This work is the Human movement of the Dao.

It is the living of a life.

It is the following of Ming, and it is the Human Way.

This is being hollow.

"Brittle Bones":

Have care for those who are hollowed but not hollow, for even as the Dao is privy to itself, we do not know.

We "straw dogs" are still nothing less than the manifest of the Dao.

To be either a vessel for violence or a carrier of compassion requires a flame.

It is good to keep the bones as hollow as a bird's, so that the workings of the Dao can flow through.

Even the densest bone holds empty space.

Even in "old age," the tendons tighten, the blood will dry in the vessels, and the muscles will waste away. This is the way of nature.

Even here, the spirits still go about their work.

One can still be open and to the Dao!

COMMENTARY

THE *DAODEJING* STATES:

"The Dao is empty, yet no vessel is left unfilled."[189]

The passage tells us that we, like the Dao, ought to be empty, that we ought to be unfettered, and we can thus realize the state of being a true human (*zhenren*). This is very good in theory. In this passage, we encounter the idea of hollowness. This is an idea that can be either positive or negative, salubrious or deleterious, curse or boon.

To be hollowed is to have something taken from you—a condition unfulfilled. To be hollow is to provide the space through which something can move with ease. To be hollow represents the physicality of emptiness.

The congress of Yin and Yang allows one to live. It is through the interaction of these two principles that we are given both form and function. This state of interplay is intrinsic and vital.

Under any circumstances, this intimate relationship between Yin and Yang can be fragile, even during easy times, but the imperative to remain hollow is ever-present. There must be open, empty space through and into which Yin and Yang can penetrate and move. By extension, all derivations of Yin and Yang, including those crucial to human existence, such as qì, blood, jīng, and shén can move freely and easily.

To be hollowed out by life's capricious circumstance is a very different thing than allowing for the fertile emptiness that is spoken to in this passage.

In the former situation, one is often shut off from their own potencies by an unbidden, embodied retelling of trauma. This easily leads to numbness or dissociation which can stunt transmutation of the person, as they live and relive the same patterns. In the latter,

---

189 Adapted from Jonathan Star, *Tao Te Ching: The Definitive Translation*, 17.

there is an emptiness which has no gravity toward fullness in itself, and can be potential for transmutation, and transmutation itself. If the person is supported throughout, though, trauma can be a fecund opportunity for profound metamorphosis. In the first, restriction of awareness and expression. In the second, a renewal and affirmation of these. Most unsettling, though, from the orientation of this text is the ability of traumatic experience to blunt or sever the connection with one's own Shén spirits as they recoil away from the world.

The hollowness encouraged in this passage, in contrast, is a space for dynamism and movement—a "whirling emptiness"[190] of being which permits a liminal fullness.

The Embodiment

The ability to embody this idea of emptiness is one of the more difficult propositions found in this text, as we are very often taught in our modern cultures that emptiness is a lack of something. In the Chinese tradition, and particularly within the Daoist iterations of it, this is not a stumbling block on the road to humaneness. It is considered a requisite, which allows movement and change to occur.Again, it is very often easier for us to be hollowed out by life than it is to be hollow within it.

At least, at first.

Much of the present text speaks to the ideas of movement, emptiness, and change, particularly in the form of transformation or mutation of one's ideas, actions, and sense of "self" in relation to the world, and being hollow is necessary according to the Chinese tradition before change, freedom of movement and openness can occur. We can revisit the practices found in the passages "Emptying the Heart," "Opening the Heart," "Reattaching the Head," and several others to see these themes in action.

To give one gross illustration on the value of being hollow, think of the lowly coiled spring. Its center is structurally hollow. This is one of the components of its design which allow it to remain relatively

---

190 "Chen." Found in Star, *Tao Te Ching: The Definitive Translation*, 106.

pliable (compared to a similar length of solid material) and which allow it to store potential energy, which can then be released under the desired conditions through its ability to rebound.

This "metaphor" is encountered repeatedly within discussions of the "internal" martial arts (e.g. taiji, bagua, neijia, and xingyi), and the principle of knowing when and how to store and release one's qì also lies at the core of much of Classical Chinese medicine (CCM).[191] All of these rest on some sense of being hollow first.

Here, we take this state of hollowness or emptiness to be more than metaphor. In the Chinese traditions, hollowness allows for freedom of movement of the qì, the blood, and the collective Shén spirits as well as a "container" for certain manifestations of jīng.

To reiterate, without hollowness, the Shén spirits, as components of the composite self cannot show themselves into the world. To be hollow in this way is necessary if we are to be free and easy and clear.

Further, since the Shén represent the numinous mandate received at birth, and which provide the first embodiment of who we will be, even in utero, the ultimate consequence of being hollowed out is that the Shén leave their abodes, the qì cannot animate the body, and the blood cannot percolate through the muscles and interstices. This is dire.

Sit quietly and comfortably. Give awareness to the spine. Feel the movement of blood and qì in and around the spine.

Are you able to recognize the coursing of the blood and qì within the area?

Note the sensations arising within both the body and the psyche as this is taking place.

Next visualize the spine as a solid, dense, or even inanimate "thing." Note how the body and the mind react to this.

Notice the rigidity and weight of the space within the spine.

This is rigidity within one of the most vital axes of our existence,

---

191 While prevalent in Classical Chinese medicine (CCM), this dynamic reading of qì as potency in potential is deemphasized in "Traditional" Chinese medicine (TCM) as it was conceived during the Cultural Revolution in China circa 1949. It is during this time period that the movement of qì within the body became very circumscribed, if not almost linear and the nature of qì "morphed" so that it became a "specific" substance. This reductive approach has never fully satisfied most scientific circles and has led to many practitioners of martial arts and Chinese medicine to eschew the concept altogether.

and inflexibility that subsequently can affect all other aspects of our being.

Then let this solidified space open up or empty. Feel the heaviness within the spine flush down beginning at the base of the skull down the spine and dissipate out of the sacrum and coccyx.

Note where the downflow of stiffness and heaviness slows or stops moving down the spine. Give awareness to this space.

It can be quite common if physical or structural conditions put undo stress on the spine and the surrounding musculature. Where possible, take steps to alleviate the morphological or postural states that allow the feeling of movement, or qì, to dam up.

If there are no immediate physical or structural conditions of stress, continue to place your attention at the site of difficulty and relax into it.

If necessary, withdraw from the exercise and approach it at another time.

Physically, work to maintain the softness and flexibility of the joints so that the movement of force and potential can more easily be directed. Stretch. Contract. Relax.

If practiced consistently one may feel a softness and a slight slackness, though not a slump. It is open and empty, but not unsupported. This is the space in which the qì can move freely or as directed by the person.[192]

To Be Humane

Recognize in others the value of similar experience, particularly when we are performing the same task. There is no one experience of opening the spine or sitting in silence. Do not take your experience to be another's experience. Hollowness allows for work for self and others.

192 In a similar manner, the hollowness implied in this passage is conducive to the reception and direction of potencies received from external sources. It is hollowness which allows us to be in the triad of Heaven, Human, and Earth. Emptiness permits the interplay between the three representative principles.

Share the experience in equanimity, but do not equate the experience. It is the sharing of common qualities within unique experiences, which most often brings us together.

Allow others to have their own hollowness of being. This will permit the fullness of life which emptiness can portend.

Do not equate being hollow with having nothing, equate it with the ability or capacity to hold the ten-thousand things which typify human life. It is never nothing; it is the deep, quiet space needed to direct all things. As the *Yijing* indicates: "The jūnzǐ (君子)[193] honors the dissolving pause [in order to] overfill emptiness."[194]

---

193 In the metaphysical sense, the junzi is the person who orders their existence in world with the foundational processes of the Dao, even if they have not attained the fully realized qualities of Sagehood. This is a state which many of us can attain which does not necessary require that one abandon or radically transmute established personal or societal patterns to the same extent as the hermit-like sagaciousness which marks the Daoist Sage.
194 Ritsema and Sabbadini, *The Original I Ching Oracle*, 288.

稚子气概:

您以什麼方式找到人類?

以及從中保留什麼?

首先,在自我中找到柔軟。並不是使人失去彈性,而是使人柔韌,靈活,頭腦清晰。

在保持對自己的這種尊重時,只有這樣,對他人的人道。

...

問候萬萬種柔軟,柔韌和常綠的東西。

Zhìzǐ Qìgài:

Nín yǐ shénme fāngshì zhǎodào rénlèi?

Yǐjí cóngzhōng bǎoliú shénme?

Shǒuxiān, zài zìwǒ zhōng zhǎodào róuruǎn. Bìng bùshì shǐ rén shīqù tánxìng, ér shì shǐ rén róurèn, línghuó, tóunǎo qīngxī.

Zài bǎochí duì zìjǐ de zhè zhǒng zūn chóng shí, zhǐyǒu zhèyàng, duì tārén de réndào.

脆骨：

但是，說我們輕鬆地接受人道是錯誤的，特別是如果其他人扼殺了我們對自發表達和自然滿足的需求。

我們可以很容易地變得自私，以便慾望會因"良好的意圖"而氾濫成風。

應該做什麼？

返回。

返回。

…

只有對存在，做事和完成的方式的認識。

Cuìgú:

Dànshì, shuō wǒmen qīngsōng de jiēshòu réndào shì cuòwù de, tèbié shì rúguǒ qítā rén èshāle wǒmen duì zì fābiǎo dá hé zìrán mǎnzú de xūqiú.

Wǒmen kěyǐ hěn róngyì dì biàn dé zìsī, yǐbiàn yùwàng huì yīn "liánghǎo de yìtú" ér fànlàn chéng fēng.

Yīnggāi zuò shénme?

Fǎnhuí.

Fǎnhuí.

...

Zhǐyǒu duì cúnzài, zuòshì hé wánchéng de fāngshì de rènshí.

On Keeping to the Human Way

"Baby's Breath":

Wherein do you find a human way?

And what to keep, therefrom?

First, find softness in the self. Not so that one loses resilience, but such that one is pliant, flexible, and clear in vision and in mind.

In keeping this regard for oneself, only then, humaneness toward others.

In truth, this is not human, as such, as much as it is a means to foster humaneness.

Greet the world with equanimity and evenness in being.

Greet each of the ten-thousand things soft, pliable, and evergreen.

"Brittle Bones":

It is natural for the human to adopt "human-ness" in both form and in function.

It is a falsehood though, to say that we easily embrace humaneness, especially if others have stifled our own need for spontaneous expression, and natural contentment.

We can very easily become selfish so that the desires will run ram-

pant and roughshod over "good intentions."

What should be done?

Return.

Return.

Over time, the course will be harder to leave, and the course will lead, as an old ox will lead the plow—no charge or challenge, only softness and persistence.

Ask the ox how it does!

If silence, ask again.

If met with silence once more—ask again, but on the other ear. The ox will tell you.

It is this Yin nature which allows the ox to precede the plow.

Then even with greatest docility, it precedes the rows.

To greet the world with equanimity is to regard things with an evenness. There is, in this place, a recognition that no thing is inherently better than another.

There is only the recognition of thusness of being, doing, and being done.

COMMENTARY

THE IDEA OF rén (人) or "humanity" consists of much more than having a human form or shape (xing) or "human" emotions. In the Chinese tradition, our occurrence as humans is seen as a boon bestowed upon each of us, which is to be acknowledged, respected, treasured, and preserved.

> The true [human, *zhenren* (真人)] acts Heaven-like while keeping his humanity, thus he has a chance to overcome Heaven, precisely by not trying to overcome it. The only thing we can do to overcome the uncontrollable is to merge with it, to become one with it, "to hide the world in the world."[195]

The Embodiment

The force of one's nature, and the drives attending it, cannot be underestimated in the face of one's own experience and "allotted time" (*ming*). Even if there is no Heaven, act as though there is. Even if there is no Divine mandate or fatal pattern within one's life, look for that which makes you Human among humans and work this as your idea of ming, as this is the same as following the Dao and being in accordance with Heaven and Earth.

In learning to breathe smoothly, quietly, and in practicing this with repetition, you are doing the Rendao, the Human Way.

In communication and quiescence, knowing when to speak and when to hold the tongue, or when to "cross the great river" (choosing one's timing for and level of engagement with others), you are working the Human way. Being among others without being subsumed by them. Holding our boundaries when necessary and allowing them to dissolve when appropriate.

195 Mercedes Valmisa, "Beyond our Control? Two Responses to Uncertainty and Fate in Early China," in Livia Kohn, (ed.), *New Visions of the Zhuangzi* (Honolulu: Three Pines Press, 2015).

In cultivating any aspect of your unfolding life, in strengthening, fostering, your capacities as a being, you are doing the Human way. And lastly, in protecting and conserving your own deep resources, notably your time and your effort, you are doing the Human way.

To Be Humane

In this passage, the humane act is to help others to recognize their own humanity.

This can be complicated in that, we are given free rein to go about the world, and there are times when we act in ways that may be harmful to others and, yet, also necessary.

Helping one to "return" to a state of humanity or humane clarity, is thus the performance of virtue par excellence. At the same time it is natural to recognize that we each must have our own Way as a Human. Openness to the Dao becomes openness to our own humaneness.

稚子气概：

修養是您對事物的熱愛。

當實踐到位時，就會有結果。

練習要輕鬆自在，但必須練習。

Zhìzǐ Qìgài:

Xiūyǎng shì nín duì shìwù de rè'ài.

Dāng shíjiàn dàowèi shí, jiù huì yǒu jiéguǒ.

Liànxí yào qīngsōng zìzài, dàn bìxū liànxí.

脆骨：

做吧！

如果您做得對，那麼您將一無所獲。

從“錯誤”開始。

沒人知道那是什麼

不過，做到這一點！

Cuìgú:

Zuò ba!

Rúguǒ nín zuò dé duì, nàme nín jiāng yīwúsuǒhuò.

Cóng "cuòwù" kāishǐ.

Méi rén zhīdào nà shì shénme bùguò.

Zuò dào zhè yīdiǎn!

On Cultivation

"Baby's Breath":

Cultivation is the devotion of your experience to a thing.

When the practice is there, there will be results.

Be free and easy with your practice, but you must practice.

"Brittle Bones":

Do it!

If you do the work right you won't be doing anything.

Begin by doing it "wrong."

No one else knows what that is, anyway

Still, do it!

COMMENTARY

CULTIVATION IN ANY form is a work in vitality, at least within Daoism. To cultivate is to tend, to guard, to keep, and to regard a thing; it is not solely about the pooling up of a thing.

Take gardening as an example. To put a seed in the soil is one thing. This is the barest dull minimum. You can prepare the soil. You can choose the proper space for the plant. You can water it. Once you set the initial conditions, the time of the first sprouting is not truly up to the gardener.

Cultivation of being is the same, except that what sprouts within each of us are the many varieties of our own internal milieu.

Fabrizio Pregadio writes:

From the point of view of the practice, "cultivating ming" (xiuming; 修命) and "nourishing ming" (yangming; 養命) are two of the most frequent positive expressions related to ming:

"If one is able to empty his Heart and to sooth his Spirit, this is how to nourish one's xing. If one is able to cherish his Essence and to care for his Breath, this is how to nourish one's ming."[196]

人能虛心棲神，所以養性也；惜精愛氣，所以養命也。

Broadly, neidan, the process of internal cultivation, acknowledges the expressions mentioned above in two main senses. In the first sense, ming should be "extended" or "prolonged" (yan, chang, etc.) by means of neidan practices. This usually means enhancing or increasing one's vital force (qì) in order to prolong one's length of life. In the second sense, cultivating ming involves two different movements: a forward (or downward) movement whereby one conforms to and complies with ming

JOHN ANDERSON

196 Fabrizio Pregadio, "Destiny, Vital Force, or Existence? On the Meanings of Ming 命 in Daoist Internal Alchemy and its Relation to Xìng 性 or Human Nature," *Daoism: Religion, History and Society* 6 (2014): 167–68.

as the course of one's life, and "follows" it (shùnsuì 順遂); and a backward (or upward) movement whereby one "returns" (fu) to the original mandate of life in accordance with the Dao. With regard to the first movement ("following ming"), we read:

The upright noble man keeps his Heart undisturbed. When he is in service, he gives advice at court; when he is not in service, he betakes himself into mountains and forests. When he dwells among riches and honors, he is not proud of himself; when he resides in poverty and humility, he does not flatter anyone. In advancing and withdrawing he is always measured; in movement and quiescence he is always proper. As he constantly follows Heaven's mandate without deception, he can be called an upright noble man.

正人君子，坦然其心。用之則陳道朝廷，不用則隱拙山林。居富貴不 驕，處貧賤不諂。進退合度，動靜合宜。常順天命而心不欺，可以為 正人君子也矣。

The *Daodejing* further advises us to:

Attain the ultimate of emptiness, guard the utmost of quiescence. The ten thousand things are brought about together: accordingly, I observe their return. Things are abounding and overflowing, but each of them reverts to its root. Reverting to the root is called quiescence, and this means returning to the mandate (ming); returning to the mandate is called constancy; knowing constancy is called brightness.

致虛極，守靜篤。萬物並作，吾以觀復。夫物芸芸，各復歸其根。 歸 根曰靜，是謂復命，復命曰常，知常曰明。

The Embodiment

Cultivation is a slow thing for most of us. It requires practice and a willingness to allocate some of our experience to the process of change. It is not about getting "better" at something, or becoming stronger, but on the recognition and distillation of change as our individual lives unfold.

To cultivate, practice.

Find a door and go through it, even if the old masters call it a side door.

Do the thing.

Refine, redefine, and abandon the experience until it simply issues forth from you as you move through it.

Let yourself unfold as just one part of a larger field of experience. In this, the world changes, and the world changes each of us in our turn.

Slow down.

Sit still.

Breathe.

Direct your qì upward, downward, and throughout the vessels and limbs.

Preserve the Yin and the Yang even as you watch them transform.

Quiet the Heart mind.

Root the Spirits and let them fly.

Talk with your Shén: they are your allies.

Find quietude in the Heart.

Find fortitude in the mind.

All of these are cultivation.

To Be Humane

Practice.

Do fully and without pretense.

Help others to find the first green impulse toward movement and clarity and help to foster this in them.

Doing the first realizes Humanness in yourself: doing the second shows others that Humanness exists in others, and by bright reflection, in themselves. This is virtue brought full-circle.

PARTING REMARKS

THE SHÉN EXISTS as both the axle and the hub. It does not move but allows for movement to happen. It is the earthly mound upon with sacred fire is built and it is the depth of the fire itself. It is both the base and the pinnacle of being.

The present text exists as an exposition of the spirit of being in the world and of having access to more than one "world." It was conceived as part of a triptych in which one might see the workings of the Hún, the Pò, and the Shén reflected in some manner. As such, this text could have arrived at any point in the order of the three, except that it couldn't, or perhaps, wouldn't.

Where *The Way of the Living Ghost* gave a glimpse onto a path that was accentuated by a dirty glint of falsehood, this text sought to "clear the orifices," to cut away the cataracts, and make the ears keen by dint of actually listening to oneself wherever one might be. This is fundamental to the Human way.

Awareness and ease are necessary to the work at hand in the next volume, which seeks to open up invisible spaces within oneself, just as the Shén and the Hún can accompany one another.

The last book in this framework will deal with topics more properly considered esoteric in their own right and will address the state of the Hún spirit as part of this process. The Hún is, after all, the spirit within us which deals with the future (and time), death and transubstantiation (it ascends to the heavens, if all goes well), and lifts up the Pò by providing the freshness and pliability needed to keep the saturnine Pò youthful and (relatively) unfettered by the physicality of the world.

The Shén as an agent of awareness, distinguished from the broader repository of existence that is each of us, as an individual spirit, must be seated if the other spirits are to come through, to have their say. In this way, it acts as an antenna and an amplifier, refining and strengthening the generally very subtle impulses of the other Shén spirits and other parts of our imaginal geography. This treatise is about awareness—an awareness of the self through an animist lens. It is both full of spirits and filled by one Spirit, which guides being. It is full of fractiousness and movements of wholeness.

Among other things, the next volume will begin to address the incompleteness of even this standpoint. For, while it is consistent to say that there is a thread of bestowed and innate nature (xing), that nature is given to the spirits. "I," as one of the central propositions of existence within modern society, is still liminal. It flashes into and out of existence—"I" flash into and out of existence. The singular Shén as a receptacle for "human-ness" utilizes its innate nature to coalesce and cohere my experience, as my self, but it isn't always so. Thus, the Hún, the Shén, and the Pò must strike their balances in many dimensions at once.

The material of the third volume will address other worlds, and other possibilities. This encompasses both those possibilities that have come to realization and also those that have not yet been formed. The Hún sees these potential places, gives us the light and clarity of vision, and, as the spirit of the wind within us, bends around obstacles. Within its pages the reader will find ideas on living talismanically, if quietly, with oneself through the Hún spirit, as well as greater recognition, reception, and recourse to rarity that the interior altars provide in both pre-heaven and post-heaven forms of spirit, in the form of the Yì and the Zhì. This is the space of the ancestors and of the earth, both realized within each person, and of the spaces of "Chaos" and "Order," even if they are of the same Mother. It is also the space in which one might hang in a state of liminality, in between worlds, gently pulled by the Pò back to earth as the Shén gives form to the futures that the Hún has explored—just as the Yin anchors the Yang so that life can unfold.

It is only that one is the elder and the other, younger.

The trick is to find out which is which and how.

294

BIBLIOGRAPHY

Adler, Joseph. "Zhu Xi's Spiritual Practice as the Basis of His Central Philosophical Concepts." *Dao: A Journal of Comparative Philosophy* 7.1 (2008): 57–79.

Allen, Sarah. *The Shape of the Turtle: Myth, Art and Cosmos in Early China.* Albany: SUNY Press, 1991.

Allione, Tsultrim. *Feeding Your Demons: Ancient Wisdom for Resolving Inner Conflict.* New York: Little, Brown & Co., 2008.

Anderson, John. *The Way of the Living Ghost.* Seattle: Revelore Press, 2019.

Andreeva, Anna and Dominic Steavu (eds.). *Transforming the Void: Embryological Discourse and Reproductive Imagery in East Asian Religions.* Leiden: Brill, 2015.

Ban, Gu. "On Humanity's Emotions and Higher Virtues: A Passage from the Chapter "Qingxing" in the *Baihu tongde lun (Discussions on the Power of Virtue in the White Tiger Hall)*." Translated by Heiner Fruehauf, 2015. https://classicalchinesemedicine.org/humanitys-emotions-higher-virtues-passage-chapter-qingxing-baihu-tongde-lun-discussions-power-virtue-white-tiger-hall-ban-gu/.

Berenstein, Elizabeth. "The Food That Helps Battle Depression." *The Wall Street Journal.* April 2, 2018.

Bertschinger, Richard, (trans.). *Daodejing: The Dao and its Energy.* (2009): https://mytaoworld.com/books/the-dao-de-jing/

Bynner, Witter ,(trans.). "To Li Bai at the Sky's End." From *300 Tang Poems* (New York: Knopf, 1920).

Chai, David. "Nothingness and Selfhood in the Zhuangzi." *Bloomsbury Handbook of Early Chinese Ethics and Philosophy*, ed. Alexus McLeod. New York: Bloomsbury Academic, 2019.

Dechar, Lorie. "Wu Shen—The Five Spirits." https://www.anewpossibility.com/wp-content/uploads/2016/06/Wu-Shen_UK-2015.pdf

De Groot, J. M. *The Religious Systems of China: Its Ancient Forms, Evolution, History and Present Aspect. Manners, Customs and Social Institutions Connected Therewith.* Vol. 5. Leiden: Brill, 1964.

Dogen. "Sansui Kyo" ("Mountains and Waters Discourse."). Translated by Kazuaki Tanahashi https://www.upaya.org/uploads/pdfs/MountainsRiversSutra.pdf

Edou, Jerome. *Machig Labdron and the Foundations of Chod.* Ithaca: Snow Lion, 1996.

Feng, H. Y. and J. K. Shryock. "The Black Magic in China Known as K'u." *Journal of the American Oriental Society* 55.1 (1935): 1–30.

Fruehauf, Heiner (trans.). "On Humanity's Emotions and Higher Virtues: A Passage from the Chapter "Qingxing" in the *Baihu tongde lun* (*Discussions on the Power of Virtue in the White Tiger Hall*); attributed to Ban Gu) fl. 1st Century CE." (2015): https://classicalchinesemedicine.org/humanitys-emotions-higher-virtues-passage-chapter-qingxing-baihu-tongde-lun-discussions-power-virtue-white-tiger-hall-ban-gu/

Fruehauf, Heiner. "All Disease Comes From the Heart: The Pivotal Role of the Emotions in Classical Chinese Medicine," (2007): www.classicalchinesemedicine.org

———. "Driving Out Demons and Snakes—Gu Syndromes: A Forgotten Clinical Approach to Chronic Parasitism," (1998): https://classicalchinesemedicine.org/wp-content/uploads/2015/10/fruehauf_drivingout.pdf

Hammer, Leon, *Dragon Rises, Red Bird Flies: Psychology and Chinese Medicine, Revised Edition.* Seattle: Eastland Press, 2005.

——— and Hamilton Rotte. *Chinese Herbal Medicine: The Formulas of Dr. John H. F. Shen.* New York: Thieme, 2012.

Harper, Donald. *Early Chinese Medical Literature: The Mawangdui Medical Manuscripts.* New York: Kegan Paul, 1998.

Henricks, Robert, (trans.). *Lao-Tzu: Te-Tao Ching: A New Translation Based on the Recently Discovered Ma-wang tui Texts.* New York: Ballantine Books, 1992.

Hinton, David. (trans.). *Chuang Tsu—The Inner Chapters.* Berkeley: Counterpoint Press, 2014.

Huang, Huayu. "Rén and Gǎntōng: Openness of Heart and the Root Of Confucianism." *Philosophy East & West* 62.4 (2012): 463–504.

Jiang, Yonglin. *The Great Ming Code: Da Ming Lu.* Seattle: University of Washington Press, 2014.

Johnson, Jerry Alan. *Daoist Magical Incantations, Hand Seals, and Star Stepping.* Pacific Grove: The International Institute of Daoist Magic, 2006.

Jung, C. G. *Contributions to Analytical Psychology.* Abington: Routledge & Kegan Paul, 1948.

Keightley, David and Henry Rosemont. *These Bones Shall Rise Again: Selected Writings on Early China.* Albany: State University of New York Press, 2014.

Kikuchi Noritaka. "The Accumulation of Crime and Punishment: The Ancient Daoist Notion of 'Inherited Burden' and its Relevancy Today." *Journal of International Philosophy* 1 (2012): 194–99.

Kohn, Livia, (ed.). *The Taoist Experience: An Anthology.* Albany: SUNY Press, 1993.

———, (ed.). *Daoist Body Cultivation: Traditional Models and Contemporary Practices.* Honolulu: University of Hawaii Press, 2006.

——— and Harold D. Roth. *Daoist Identity: History, Lineage, and Ritual.* Honolulu: University of Hawaii Press, 2002.

Larre, Claude and Elisabeth Rochat de la Vallee (trans.). *The Heart in Lingshu* Chapter 8. London: Monkey Press, 2004.

——— (trans.). *Rooted in Spirit: The Heart of Chinese Medicine.* Barrytown: Station Hill Press, 1995.

Legge, James. (Trans.) *The I Ching.* Sacred Books of the East, vol. 16, 1899. Internet Sacred Text Archive. https://www.sacred-texts.com/ich/index.htm.

Lewis, Clive. S. *The Problem of Pain.* New York: Harper Collins, 2001.

Liu, Ming. "Healing Apprenticeship—Class 7 Possession: TCM and Possession Part One: Basic View." www.dayuancircle.org.

———. "Healing Apprenticeship—Class 8 Possession: TCM and Possession Part Two: Common Prevention." dayuancircle.org.

———. "Healing Apprenticeship—Class 9 Possession: TCM and Possession Part Three: Forms of Treatment." dayuancircle.org.

———. "Healing Apprenticeship—Class 10 Possession: TCM and Possession Part Four: Earth Spirits." dayuancircle.org.

———. "Healing Apprenticeship—Class 11 Possession: TCM and Possession Part Five: Water Spirits." dayuancircle.org

Liu, Xiang. *Shuoyuan* 說苑 (*The Garden of Stories*). In public domain. http://chinesenotes.com/shuoyuan.html.

Liu Yiming. *Cultivating the Tao: Taoism and Internal Alchemy*. Translated by Fabrizio Pregadio. Mountain View: Golden Elixir Press, 2013.

Liu, Yousheng. *Let the Radiant Yang Shine Forth: Lectures on Virtue*. Translated by Sabine Wilms and Liu Zuozhi. Freeland: Happy Goat, 2017.

Low-Beer, S. "The Superior Physician: Medical Practice as Seen Through the Yijing's Junzi, Part 2," (2009): www.classicalchinesemedicine.org

Maciocia, Giovani. *Foundations of Chinese Medicine: A Comprehensive Text*, 3rd Edition. London: Churchill-Livingstone, 2015.

Major, John S, et al. (trans). *The Huainanzi: A Guide to the Theory and Practice of Government in Early Han China*. New York: Columbia University Press, 2010.

Maspero, Henri. *Taoism and Chinese Religion*. Translated by Frank A. Kierman Jr. Amherst: University of Massachusetts Press, 1981.

Meulenbeld, Mark. "Daoist Modes of Perception: 'Registering' the Living Manifestations of Sire Thunder, and Why Zhuang Zi is Relevant." *Daoism: Religion, History and Society* 8 (2016): 35–91.

Michael, Thomas. "Mountains and Early Daoism in the Writings of Ge Hong." *History of Religions*. 56.1 (2016): 23–54.

Pregadio, Fabrizio. "Yin and Yang." Golden Elixir Press, 2019: https://www.goldenelixir.com/taoism/yin_and_yang.html.

———. "Creation and Its Inversion: Cosmos, Human Being, and Elixir in the "Cāntóng qì [參同契]" (The Seal of the Unity of the Three)," 186–211. In Andreeva and Steavu, (eds)., *Transforming the Void* (Leiden: Brill, 2015).

———. "Destiny, Vital Force, or Existence? On the Meanings of Ming 命 in Daoist Internal Alchemy and its Relation to Xing 性 or Human Nature." *Daoism: Religion, History and Society* 6 (2014): 157–218.

——— (ed.). *The Encyclopedia of Taoism.* London: Routledge, 2008

Puett, M. "Sages, the Past, and the Dead—Death in the *Huainanzi*," 225–49. In Amy Olberding and Philip J. Ivanhoe, (eds.), *Mortality in Traditional Chinese Thought* (Albany: SUNY Press, 2011).

Reid, Dan G. *The Thread of Dao: Unraveling Early Daoist Oral Traditions in Guan Zi's Purifying the Heart-Mind (Bai Xīn), Art of the Heart-Mind (Xīn Shu), and Internal Cultivation (Nei Ye).* Montreal: Center Ring, 2019.

Ritsema, Rudolf and Shantena Augusto Sabbadini. *The Original I Ching Oracle or The Book of Changes.* London: Watkins, 2018.

Rossi, Eliza. *Shen—Psycho-emotional Aspects of Chinese Medicine.* London: Elsevier, 2007.

Roth, Harold D. *A Companion to Angus Graham's Chuang Tzu.* Honolulu: University of Hawai'i Press, 2003.

Schipper, Kristofer and Karen C. Duval (trans.). *The Taoist Body.* Berkeley: University of California Press, 1993.

Schlosser, David B. "The Five Virtues of Confucius": http://www.dbschlosser.com/five-virtues-of-confucius/

Stanley-Baker, M. "Palpable Access to the Divine: Daoist Medieval Massage, Visualisation and Internal Sensation." *Asian Medicine* 7 (2012): 101–27.

Star, Jonathan (trans.). *Tao Te Ching: The Definitive Translation.* New York: Tarcher, 2003.

Suzuki, Daisetsu Teitoro and Paul Carus. *The Canon of Reason and Virtue: (Lao-tze's Tao Teh King) Chinese and English.* La Salle: Open Court, 1913. http://www.sacred-texts.com/tao/crv/index.htm

Tran, Loan Guylaine (trans.). "Jing Xīn Shen Zhou: Purifying the Heart Mantra" Wudang Five Immortals Temple (2020): http://fiveimmortals.com/the-eight-great-incantation/

Unschuld, Paul (ed.). *Huang Di Nei Jing Su Wen: An Annotated Translation of Huang Di's Inner Classic—Basic Questions.* Berkeley: University of California Press, 2011.

Valmisa, Mercedes. "Beyond our Control? Two Responses to Uncertainty and Fate in Early China." In Livia Kohn (ed.), *New Visions of the Zhuangzi* (Honolulu: Three Pines Press, 2015).

Wang, Fengyi. *Twelve Characters—A Transmission of Wang Fengyi's Teachings.* Translated by Sabine Wilms. Corbett: Happy Goat, 2014.

Wei Haiquan, Hiromitsu Taniguchi, and Liu Ruoxin. "Chinese Myths and Legends for Tianchi Volcano Eruptions." *Northeast Asian Studies* 6 (2002): 191–200.

Wilmont, Dennis. *The Five Phases of Acupuncture in the Classical Texts.* Marshfield: Willmountain Press, 2009.

Ziporyn, Brook. *Zhuangzi: The Complete Writings.* Cambridge: Hackett, 2020.

About the Author

John Anderson received his Master of Sciences degree from the Florida College of Integrative Medicine in 2009 and his Doctorate in Acupuncture and Oriental Medicine in 2012 from the Oregon College of Oriental Medicine. He has taught all aspects of Traditional Chinese Medicine in schools across the country. He has written on many topics including: Eastern philosophy, Chinese medicine, herbal medicine, and disability studies.

He has been studying and working with the Yijing for nearly twenty years, both as a divinatory system and as a shorthand for understanding the Earth and the broader cosmos around and within each of us.

In his spare time, he can be found smoking cigars, talking with ghosts of various sorts, and peering into the future, though he rarely tells anyone what he sees.

He currently resides in Florida.

About the Series

The Folk Necromancy in Transmission series examines the folk magical expressions and interrelations of the histories, philosophies, and practices of spirit conjuration, ghost-lore, eschatology, charm-craft, demonology, and the mass of rituals, protocols, and beliefs signalled by the terms "nigromancy," "necromancy," and their various equivalents in traditions across the world.

Here we take the canonical and reveal the folkloric expression; here the historical text inspires new practice and discourse. This series will not simply chart the print history of grimoires, or their socio-political context, but explore their actual magical usage. Within this exploration comes discourse on and with those traditions, extant or extinct, deemed 'necromantic' that are passed through oral transmission.

Raising the dead, we acknowledge the raising of necromancy itself, for it is still the breath of the reader that gives new life to the Dead from the bones of old Books. This is a folk necromancy that is at once extant and revived, inspired and yet-to-be. Here we walk hand-in-hand with the patrons of this particular Art.

OPENING THE VERMILLION SPIRIT
WAS TYPESET BY JOSEPH UCCELLO.
THE TYPEFACES:
JJANNON, JJANNON DISPLAY,
ADOBE FANGSONG STD,
KAZURAKI SP2N, GT AMERICA,
XINGKAI SC, GRAEBENBACH,
SKOLAR PE, PINGFANG HK, & LIHEI.

CPSIA information can be obtained
at www.ICGtesting.com
Printed in the USA
BVHW011438090322
630900BV00025B/355

9 781947 544307